# SMART WOMEN,
# SMART MONEY

# SMART WOMEN, SMART MONEY

## LIVE THE LIFE YOU WANT

JOAN BAKER

ALLEN&UNWIN

Joan welcomes comments on this and her other books. She can be contacted at: jbaker@wealthcoaches.net

First published in 2004


Allen & Unwin
83 Alexander Street
Crows Nest NSW 2065
Australia
Phone: (61 2) 8425 0100
Fax: (61 2) 9906 2218
Email: info@allenandunwin.com
Web: www.allenandunwin.com

National Library of Australia
Cataloguing-in-Publication entry:

Baker, Joan.
Smart women, smart money: live the life you want.

ISBN 1 74114 364 0.

1. Women—Finance, Personal. I. Title.

332.02402082

Set in 10.5/13 pt ArrusBT by Midland Typesetters, Maryborough, Victoria
Printed by Griffin Press, Netley, South Australia

10 9 8 7 6 5 4 3 2 1

# CONTENTS

# INTRODUCTION

Women today value and expect financial independence. Whether a woman is single and child-free, responsible for bringing up children or supporting aged parents, in a committed relationship or about to retire, the importance of security and control over her finances is paramount: it can bring a sense of peace, a feeling of satisfaction and the knowledge that she can remain in control of her own life.

But such a situation does not happen automatically. The foundations need to be laid as early as possible, goals set and strategies adopted. Particularly at a time when many women will remain single for a large part of their lives—through choosing not to marry or partner, or because of divorce or death of a spouse—smart women need to take control of their financial futures and shape them to suit their own goals, dreams and ideals.

Women are often accused of the 'Cinderella' syndrome where they expect to be 'rescued' by Prince Charming or other heroes who exist only in fairytales. But long gone are the days when women relinquished control of their own finances at marriage, and were supported for the rest of their lives by a dutiful and hard-working husband. Maybe such a time was largely a myth anyway—many women throughout the last century and earlier faced the harsh reality of having to support a family even when they had a husband in work. And many—for numerous reasons—could never count on the income of their family's so-called 'breadwinner'.

In those days, however, governments made certain assumptions: the husband would earn a family wage; the wife had no need to work. Single mothers, single women and divorced or separated women simply didn't come into this equation.

Now things have changed—at least on the surface. Now

women have the chance to work and build a career, as well as access to the same social security net and the same legal rights to their financial and material assets as men.

However, women still face an uphill climb when it comes to achieving equal promotion and the same level of wages as men, and many still have to juggle the demands of motherhood or other caring responsibilities with work commitments. Reaching the so-called 'glass ceiling' and a broken career path are further realities for most women. And let's face it, many women approach work differently: they are choosing to combine work and motherhood because that's what they want to do.

Clearly, women's financial needs are different, so they have to look at money and its management differently. Many of the same principles apply, but the whole concept of money management needs to be examined in a different way. That's what we've set out to do in this book: approach money, its management and the whole question of financial independence and security from a woman's point of view.

This book is for all women—young and old, single and partnered, with or without children or other caring responsibilities, employed or self-employed. And it is about more than money—which, after all, is simply a means to achieve a better life and a sense of satisfaction and happiness. It is about taking control of your life, through your financial management and your attitude to money. And it is about doing it from a woman's perspective.

# PART I

# THE MONEY MINDSET

# 1
# WHY IT'S DIFFERENT FOR WOMEN

As women, we have more opportunities and options today than at any time in history. We earn more and have more money than ever before. Men no longer automatically own and control women's assets. We are legally entitled to continue working after marriage and to keep our jobs even when we have children—something our grandmothers and even some of our mothers were unable to do. In law (if not always in practice), we are entitled to equal pay for equal work. The old barriers and stereotypes are slowly eroding. Women are increasingly found in senior roles in all areas of work and society. Many small businesses have been established and are owned by women—a trend which continues. In many ways, the world is a great deal fairer than it used to be and there have been many changes in legislation that make it easier for women to succeed and be independent. We have seen huge changes for the better over the last century. It might not be perfect, but this is probably the best time in history to be a woman!

However, some things don't change for women. When it comes to financial independence, there are several factors that make women different and make it much more difficult for them to take care of themselves financially.

## BIOLOGY

Childbirth and childrearing pose challenges for women's financial independence that men don't (usually) face. Many of these challenges are emotional, but others are very practical, such as the time it takes out of your paid working life. Women commonly lose several years of working life giving birth to and taking care of their children. This obviously has a big effect on earnings. It can also affect a woman's opportunities for promotion and progress in her career. Even with the increasing availability of childcare and changing social attitudes, childrearing is still mainly a woman's role. And women who have children often pay a big price financially.

## TIME

Time is not on women's side. Women live longer, which may appear to be a good thing. However, it is difficult to earn money in one's later years, and if we are living longer we need more wealth to take us through our old age in comfort and security. Later life can be very expensive if you want it on your terms. Whether they've been married or not, women are likely to be alone in their later years and will almost certainly be on a single income for some time. Life expectancy continues to rise and many women today should cheerfully expect to be still spending well into their eighties.

Women are usually slightly younger than their husbands or partners. Added to longer life expectancy, this means that women can expect to be widowed or on their own for over a decade, on average. This is frequently a recipe for poverty, as the income is often halved (or may cease) but the expenses continue much as before. Women need to plan in the knowledge that they may be alone for many years in later life.

While women outlive men, time is against us in the wealth creation stakes. Women on average are out of the workforce for longer and more frequently than men, and therefore earn less, but they also live longer, which means the smaller amount of money that women do earn has to last for longer. More than 85 years (and rising) is a lot of spending time to plan for.

## FAMILY STRUCTURES

Women today can no longer expect that the men in their lives will take care of them financially, and most no longer want this.

Many women are choosing not to marry at all, and it's hardly news that almost half of all marriages now end in divorce. Divorce is expensive—your assets could be halved overnight. Even though changes in legislation have attempted to make separation a fairer deal for women, we typically emerge with a lower standard of living and greater financial problems. Most women will have custody of any children from the relationship and all of the financial responsibilities that go with that care. Many will have been out of the workforce or working only part-time, so will face all the expected difficulties of resuming a career. Women may find themselves forced to return to the work-force after long absences and often poorly skilled—this is not a recipe for high income. Child custody not only brings expense but also has work-limiting aspects. Single parents are over-whelmingly female—and single parents find it very difficult to get ahead financially.

When couples divorce, statistics have shown that men's standard of living rises and women's drop in most cases. This is because of the earning power that men continue to have when the relationship is over. The law goes some way to addressing these anomalies, but women still carry most of the ongoing financial disadvantage and we need to plan our finances with this in mind.

Women need to plan, earn, save and invest as if no one else was ever going to contribute to their financial well-being or security. Life needs to be organised so that it is financially sustainable—no matter what happens.

## EARNINGS

Women earn less. Despite equal pay legislation, women continue to earn less than men. Women who are in part-time or casual work are even worse affected. All of these above factors impact on the overall amount of money that women earn and limit their ability to save and invest. Financial security is all about saving and investing—that's how wealth and financial independence are created.

The basics of managing your money effectively are very

simple: you need some income and you have to consume less than you earn. You have to create a surplus, save it and invest it to create financial independence.

> It is even more important for women to grasp and apply the concept of investment early and effectively if they have lower earnings to begin with.

## EXPECTATIONS

The future is likely to remain much the same for today's women. Welfare payments are unlikely to ever be more than minimal. Careers and employment will remain uncertain and subject to great upheavals from time to time, so money in reserve and developing career-resilience should be priorities. Skill requirements for well-paying work are likely to continue to rise, so women who don't invest in themselves will be at an increasing disadvantage. Property will be even more highly priced in the future, so if we want to be comfortably accommodated we will need to save and invest. We are likely to continue to be personally responsible for the greater part of our own retirement planning, so to have freedom and security in later life we will have to create that wealth ourselves.

## SMART WOMAN STRATEGIES

A smart woman knows the facts and understands the implications of some of the statistics concerning women and money:

- ♀ She would face reality about her prospects for taking care of herself financially (financial independence), with or without a partner.
- ♀ She would decide that she is going to take charge of her finances from now on—and become financially fit for the life she expects to have.

- ♀ She would plan around the above factors—treat them as if they were real and take steps to improve the odds in her favour.
- ♀ She would change her expectations and her attitude if they were holding her back.

# 2 WOMEN'S FINANCIAL MINDSET

Factors like biology and lifespan certainly mean women need to approach their financial management differently. However, some of the other factors which can challenge our financial well-being are more subtle. They have to do with how we have traditionally thought about ourselves and about money. In the past, girls were sometimes brought up differently and received different messages regarding their expectations about money and financial independence. Some women have developed attitudes and beliefs that have prevented them from making good decisions about money. All of us can create barriers and obstacles to financial independence—hurdles that exist only in our heads but are very real nonetheless. Our attitudes influence everything we do. They determine what information we pay attention to, what decisions we make and what habits we have.

> How many knights in shining armour have you seen recently? It's time to stop waiting for knights and princes—and to become a warrior princess!

Many of the women I've worked with have considered that taking care of themselves financially was not their responsibility. They assumed their partner, and prior to that their parents, would take care of them. In my experience, this is the biggest attitudinal problem many women have.

Largely due to social conditioning, women have a tendency to put the needs of others first; devoting time, effort and resources to other family members and expecting to be taken care of in return.

Women often act on this basis without ever stopping to question its relevance to them and their future security.

This means many women have not invested in themselves or their careers, expecting someone else to support them. Others suffer mishaps like redundancy or divorce and don't have the money or skills to get back on their feet because they have made no provision for these sorts of life events. Some older women cannot retire as they do not have enough to live on without working—they have no accumulated savings and investments or have relied on a partner who is either no longer around or who has done a poor job. Others live constrained lives, worrying about their future and unsure about what action to take. I come across many women who admit to a feeling of unease about their financial future but aren't sure what they should be doing about it. Ignorance is definitely *not* bliss when it comes to your financial security and independence.

It doesn't have to be like this! Women of all ages should be living wonderful lives and feeling very optimistic about their financial future. Any woman can make sure that she can take care of herself financially no matter what happens.

So what are some of the things that are stopping women?

Well, let's look first at how money was dealt with in your home. A generation or two ago, money was rarely discussed. Many women stayed at home, got housekeeping money and made it go as far as they could. All the really important money decisions were made by Dad. While some women worked, it was often for 'pin' money, or for family 'extras' like holidays. There was still a strong belief—reinforced in the postwar years—that a woman's 'place' was in the home. Perhaps there was 'never enough' money. It is within your family of origin that you developed your own set of attitudes about money.

Until recently, school taught us very little about money and personal financial management. Teachers, who earned fixed and secure salaries, exhorted us to learn our lessons and get a steady 'pensionable' job. Let's face it: the school system generally does not provide much support for learning the basics of financial self-reliance or encouraging the kinds of activities—like entrepreneurship—that lead to wealth creation. And traditionally girls were excluded or discouraged from taking the 'real' subjects that would make the boys successful in later life—Maths, Commerce and Physics—and encouraged to study more appropriate subjects like Home Economics and Typing.

The culture in which we live also transmits very strong messages about money. Many people with strong religious backgrounds have been taught that 'money is the root of all evil'. Some grow up in a family where it is assumed that a girl will marry a man who will 'take care' of her for the rest of her life. Many of us grew up in times or places where the roles of females were ordained—boys could become whatever they chose; girls had very few choices that were approved. However, things have changed a great deal over the last few decades and the way we were taught to see money *may* be very inappropriate for the world we now live in. It is important to be aware of your mindset, and to be able to challenge and change it if it is getting in the way. Smart women choose a mindset that helps rather than hinders.

Money is a very emotional topic. We have very strong feelings about money because of all the different things it represents. We all desire wealth and its power to change our lives for the better. We can be jealous and envious of those who have wealth. We fear money because of all of the feelings we remember which attach to money, and because of arguments about it. We crave the independence it can bring but we are often fearful of it as well. Perhaps we won't be loved if we are too able and too independent?

Money is linked to many of our feelings about competence and ability and success. Many women have very ambivalent feelings about achievement. We may not be popular if we achieve better than brothers, lovers and partners. We may threaten, and that is not our (traditional) role. We might 'over-achieve' in terms of our family and background and that might mean that we no longer fit in. Many women feel that they will be unattractive to potential partners if they are too successful and independent—and money is a measure of success.

No doubt there are elements of truth in all of these fears—they would hardly be so strong and so prevalent if they had no basis in fact. Women have always been encouraged to appear weaker and more dependent than men. This might have worked when they moved from their father's house to their husband's, but it's not going to work now! But look at the price that women pay! If women feel that they need to be 'useless' with money and unsuccessful in other ways in order to get what they want, they are setting themselves up for very difficult times financially. Women today are highly likely to be single for long periods, they are likely to be separated and divorced, they are likely to be single parents and they are likely to live for a long time—alone. If you have a set of beliefs and attitudes that is conspiring to make you poor with money, then that is a set of beliefs and attitudes that you need to change—fast!

> *It's impossible to achieve anything that you cannot imagine yourself doing.*

The reason that your underlying attitudes and beliefs are so important is that they are so powerful in determining what you do. When I work with people about their money they are often really keen and hungry to learn all the 'hard' stuff about money—all that difficult terminology and those calculations that they think are the secret to successful personal finance.

But it's the 'soft' stuff about finance that is difficult—the attitudes and the habits and the mindsets. You can learn all of the 'hard' stuff, but you will never be successful if your own mind and your own behaviour are working against you.

## SMART WOMAN STRATEGIES

A smart woman would spend some time thinking about her attitudes to and feelings about money.

- She would see whether she can identify what is holding her back.

- ♀ She would write down her memories and attitudes about money and see what they are telling her—what is stopping her doing what is right for her?
- ♀ She would talk to family members or friends about her beliefs and feelings—they might have some interesting insights about her upbringing and her mindset about money, success and independence.

# 3
# MONEY BAGGAGE

The things we tell ourselves about money are very important: every day we are 'programming' ourselves for action. We have thoughts, we make assumptions and we tell ourselves stories. We remember things we heard parents, teachers and family members say. Together, they form a mindset that we have about money—a collection of beliefs, assumptions and attitudes. Unfortunately, many of them have no basis in fact.

Don't under-estimate the importance of what you are telling yourself about money because it will have a powerful impact on you. It doesn't matter what tape you're playing—you can always put a new one in. Smart women start to *listen* to the tape they are playing. They listen for all those thoughts that are hindering their progress with money. Catch the thought and challenge it. Ask yourself whether it is helping or hindering you. Notice the way you are programming yourself. It is often interesting to see whether you can remember whose voice you are hearing—where did you pick up this bit of conditioning? And how well has the person in question managed his or her finances?

You might, for example, find yourself thinking: 'Money won't buy you happiness'. Challenge the thought:

*Who said it?*
*What does she know?*
*Do I believe it's true?*
*Will money stop me from being happy?*
*Do I have to be poor to be happy?*
*Couldn't I have some money as well as being happy?*

*Would I rather be unhappy and poor or unhappy with some funds?*

It doesn't seem to make much sense as a guiding belief for your life when you challenge it like this, does it?

Each of us has our own particular set of money baggage—depending on our upbringing and education, and even the people we associate with as an adult. You are dragging your beliefs and ideas around with you and they may be getting in the way of what you need to do to become financially independent. The first step is awareness—if you don't even know what your money mindset is, you are being influenced subconsciously. It is hard to challenge and change anything that you are oblivious to. So start to listen to the thoughts about money that flit through your mind. You may well find that you have a big pile of money baggage that you need to gather up and get rid of—it could be lying there in your way every day, blocking you as you try to get your finances in order. How much energy are you wasting, climbing over that pile every day?

Rather than erasing a belief you are questioning, it is much easier to replace it with a more helpful belief. When you catch yourself programming yourself with unhelpful thoughts, choose a new belief or attitude that will help you get on the right track and move from being stupid with money to being smart. You may have been thinking in one way about money—now you can decide to think in another way.

Below is a set of the unhelpful things I hear women say about money. Smart women who do clever things with their money have a set of beliefs and attitudes that are very different. When you find yourself saying or thinking something from the old set of beliefs, challenge it and then choose something from the new set to replace it with.

## OLD SET OF BELIEFS: 'MONEY IS THE ROOT OF ALL EVIL'

*What is evil about money?*
*Uncle Jim has money and he's very good to our family.*

*Money is neither good nor bad; it's what you do with it that counts.*
*If I had more money, I could do very good things for my children, my parents and my wider family.*

| Old set of baggage and blocking beliefs | New set of assumptions and affirmations |
|---|---|
| Money is dirty. | Wealth is good. |
| Money is the 'root of all evil'. | I can do good things with money. |
| Money won't buy you happiness. | I can be happy and financially independent. |
| Money won't buy you love. | I can be loved and financially independent. |
| It's not my responsibility. | It isn't anyone else's responsibility. |
| Some day my prince will come. | I'll be fine even without a partner. |
| I am waiting to be rescued. | I am in charge. |
| I shouldn't have to do this. | I like knowing I can take care of myself. |
| Money stuff is too hard. | It can't be hard—men can do it! |
| I'm too dumb. | I can learn anything I want to. |
| I'm too young to bother. | It is OK for me to succeed. |
| I'm too old to make any difference. | It is right for me to earn good money. |
| I was never any good at Maths. | I should be paid what I am worth. |
| I am not smart with money. | I can learn whatever I need to know to achieve financial independence. |
| I'm not educated enough. | I will plan to be better off. |
| Money is 'his' job. | I can take care of myself financially. |
| Nice girls don't talk about money. | I am a grown up and I am in charge of my finances. |
| I'm afraid of making a mistake. | I am smart enough to become good with money. |
| The government will take care of me. | I'm well educated and I'll learn. |
| I won't be loved if I'm too smart, too successful, too rich. | I'll be even more lovable when I am smart with money. |
| It takes money to make money. | Investment is for everyone. |
| Investment is for rich people. | I am the perfect age to start. |

| Old set of baggage and blocking beliefs | New set of assumptions and affirmations |
| --- | --- |
| | I will support myself to make better decisions about money.<br>I will learn to invest to make money.<br>It's OK to ask for help, to make some mistakes, and learn. |

## SMART WOMAN STRATEGIES

A smart woman would examine her set of beliefs, attitudes, assumptions, mindsets and myths about money.

- ♀ She would check her set of attitudes and beliefs about money.
- ♀ She would challenge her thinking.
- ♀ She would discard any thoughts that are hindering her.
- ♀ She would choose a new set of attitudes and beliefs.
- ♀ She would start acting as if she believes in the new set.

# PART II

# YOUR FINANCIAL POSITION

# 4
# WHY YOUR MONEY MATTERS

Financial independence is about having enough money to take care of yourself. It's about being self-sufficient—able to earn the money you need to live without being dependent on someone else. Being smart with money is about making sure that your money works as hard as you do and will last as long as you do. Financial independence is about not having to rely on others—whether the state, a partner or wider family members—to take care of you. It is about having enough money to continue to make decisions about your own lifestyle for as long as you live. Being financially fit for life is a great space to be in. At best, it means that you will have many more choices and more security than if you cannot take care of yourself on your own. You will, for example, have far more choice about where you live and how you live each day. At worst, if 'bad' things happen, you will be secure in the knowledge that you can take care of things for yourself. Should you have relationship or health concerns, for example, you will be able to afford advice, support and care during a difficult period.

*Marama's husband died last year. Jim was only 55. It was a sudden death and there had been no signs of ill-health. Two of the children are still at university and the youngest is still in school. There's still $250,000 to pay on the mortgage—it's a nice home and they had increased the mortgage to redo the kitchen. It's beautiful but they went a bit (a lot!) over the budget. Jim had a good job and the family had lived a great life. Now Marama must find a job—and she's been out of the workforce for nearly ten years. Happily, life insurance will cover most of* *the mortgage so they won't have to sell the house—it's just as well the bank insisted on the insurance as they didn't have any. But what about everything else? And how will Marama earn enough to build up retirement savings as well as take care of the kids?*

Women who I work with often get a nasty shock when a partner dies. Frequently there is much less in the 'kitty' than they were led to believe. The death of a loved one is a big enough shock without finding out that you may be poor as well—the family home may have to be sold, for example. This can mean moving away from family and friends if it is in an expensive area or moving out of the district altogether.

Again, when a relationship breaks down, many of my women clients find that the realities are harsh. There may be fewer assets to divide than they believed. This is often the case if there is a business involved—it may not be doing as well as the woman has been led to believe or the man may have been 'salting' money away elsewhere in anticipation of leaving. That money can be very hard to track down.

*Donna is only 30. She's run ragged as she's trying to hold down a full-time job and look after three small children—or, rather, pay for them to be looked after. She hardly sees them and when she does she's exhausted. Donna feels she must work as there are debts to repay. Her partner, Dave, has left. He got very depressed when his fledgling business started to fail after they lost a big contract. They borrowed a lot of money using the house for security so that had to be sold. They still owe creditors money and Donna is determined to repay it. She had no idea things were as bad as they were until Dave broke down and left. Donna is determined to rebuild her finances—and equally determined that she will never be 'in the dark' about her money again.*

Ignorance is no defence. Women in relationships are jointly responsible for the family finances. It is nothing short of lunacy to leave this entirely up to your partner—after all, it is your money too. And it is your life and lifestyle that will be in ruins if you discover too late the true state of affairs. And you may have great difficulty re-establishing your livelihood—a common situation for many women who have been out of the workforce caring for children. He may have little difficulty re-establishing himself in another job or business; she may find that she's lucky to be able to get any work at all and that may be at minimum wage level. It's a big price to pay for having your head in the sand about your finances.

In some ways, it is easier to describe the effects of dependence than independence. Dependence is about having few or no choices: no choice about where you live; no choice about how you live; no choice about who cares for you if you are in need of care; no choice about the healthcare that you receive—if you can get any at all. It is almost impossible to be poor and independent. If you have dependants—children or ageing parents—your choices will be limited even further if you find you are very strapped for money. When women find they have to move, children's schooling is upset; in addition to the upheaval and loss they have already experienced, they may lose friends and all of their familiar world. It's a huge price to pay for abdicating your responsibilities to your finances.

Women I work with tend to point out that the worst thing about financial dependence is giving away their decision-making authority. Most women want to decide for themselves where they will live, who they will associate with, what they will do with their time, where they will go, what kind of entertainment they will enjoy and how they will live their lives. We have very few of these choices if we are financially dependent. We end up in a position of having to be grateful for what little we can get rather than deciding about and choosing what we want. It can be virtually impossible to re-establish the lifestyle you had—you may well have run out of years to earn the necessary money; you may have been out of the workforce far too long, even if you had good skills once; or you may be so burdened with life as a single parent that you haven't the time or the energy to even try. It is so much smarter to avoid having to come back from this position. And in a financial sense, it *can* be easily avoided. (The personal hurt is another matter.)

Financial self-sufficiency and independence are very healthy choices to make—irrespective of your relationship status. You may be lucky enough to be in a happy marriage or partnership. Hopefully, your financial independence would be in no danger of disappearing even if you were unfortunate enough for the relationship to end. Whether you are in a relationship or not, or whether you hope or expect to be in a relationship in the future, it is in your interests to consider your financial destiny as a separate issue.

> It is never too early and never too late to move in the direction of financial independence.

No matter what your circumstances regarding age or current wealth, you can start making choices and taking steps today that will make you more financially independent for the future.

It is so easy to look back and see what we should have done in the past. There will not be a woman reading this who has not said, 'If I knew then what I know now!' However, we need to apply this sort of thinking to our future, after all, that's where we'll be living. The future is never certain but there are some things that we can be sure of: that we will need money; that we will be better off in the future if we do the right things today; and that if we want things to be different it is up to us. Consider the things you could have done differently over recent years that would have made you much more financially independent today. How would life be better today if you had made different choices a decade ago? What choices are you making today that will impact on your financial position in the future?

Financial independence is all about ensuring that you continue to have choices. It means that you can keep calling the shots in your own life irrespective of what happens around you. Financial independence matters because it is the only way that you get to live your life in the way *you* choose.

## SMART WOMAN STRATEGIES

A smart woman would resolve to 'take charge' of her financial future from today. This isn't just about money—it's about choosing to be able to make decisions about the rest of your life. A smart woman would ask herself some hard questions about the future:

*When will I be able to 'retire' or work less?*
*How much will I have to live on?*
*What do I want to be able to do?*
*How do I want to live?*
*Will I have enough money to do it 'my way'?*
*Can I pay for long-term care for myself?*
*Can I pay for care for my parents, if necessary?*
*If I am alone, will I have 'enough'?*
*If my relationship ends, how will I fare financially?*
*If things continue as they are, what does my future look like?*
*Have I enough for an emergency?*

# 5
# YOUR FINANCIAL POSITION NOW

Before you make any big decisions or dramatic changes, it's a good idea to know where you're starting from. What do you have to play with? You are about to embark on a lifelong journey in taking charge of your personal finances, so what is in your toolkit right now?

A very good way of auditing your current position about money is to think in terms of KASH (or *KA$H*). KASH stands for:

*knowledge;*
*attitudes;*
*skills; and*
*habits.*

In other words, it is about:

*how much you know about your money (knowledge);*
*the attitudes you are carrying about money;*
*the skills you have to manage or earn money; and*
*your habits in terms of money management.*

You have already looked at the attitudes you have inherited—and probably chosen some new ones. But you will also want to audit your money habits and your levels of knowledge about your money and skill in handling it.

Starting with knowledge, have a look at what you know about your own financial position. Part of this includes looking at what you are worth now and where your wealth is—in other words, a *net worth statement*.

Doing a net worth statement is simple. All you have to do is write down everything that you own and subtract from that everything that you owe. What you are trying to do is figure out how much you would have if you cashed up everything today—your net worth. Whether you are single or in a relationship, I believe you should do this *as if* you were on your own—because you may well be one day. Your partner's money is *not* yours, despite how you may be living today. If anything happens to your relationship, voluntarily or not, your financial position is likely to alter. Being realistic about your finances includes understanding what your financial position is—*on your own.*

Here is an example of Isabel's net worth statement:

| | | |
|---|---|---|
| *Assets* | | |
| *House* | *$380,000* | |
| *Rental property* | *$200,000* | |
| *Savings* | *$10,000* | |
| | | *$590,000* |
| *Liabilities* | | |
| *Mortgage* | *$295,000* | |
| *Mortgage on rental property* | *$180,000* | |
| *Credit card* | *$6,500* | |
| | | *$481,500* |
| *Net worth (Assets – Liabilities)* | | *$108,500* |

If you knew Isabel, you might think she was very wealthy—she lives in her own home and runs her own company. However, when you take away the debts (liabilities) Isabel has, her net worth is actually quite low. I have omitted all the small stuff like her five-year-old car for the sake of simplicity. I think it is a good idea to leave assets that lose their value (like cars) out of your net worth statement anyway—they clutter up your statement and encourage you to think of these things as investments. They are not.

You can easily prepare your own net worth statement. These are the most important headings:

**Assets (what you *own*)**

*Home*
*Shares*
*Investment property*
*Savings*
*Superannuation*

**Liabilities (what you *owe*)**

*Home mortgage*
*Investment property mortgage*
*Credit card*
*Car loan*
*Unpaid bills*

***Total assets – Total liabilities = Net worth***

You may own some other assets like jewellery, sports equipment or works of art. I don't usually advise people to include them unless they are extremely valuable. They complicate your net worth statement, their realisable value is often low or uncertain (even if you paid a lot for them) and they are often difficult to sell. I wouldn't even encourage you to think of these things as assets or investments unless they are very valuable. When you are deciding what value to give to your assets, you should ask yourself what you would be likely to get for them if you sold them tomorrow—at fair market value. If in doubt, take the lower number!

It is relatively simple to do your net worth statement if you are single. You may find that you will need to seek advice about the value of some things—for example, the value of your home may have changed considerably since you bought it and you may not have a good idea of its worth. You do not need every valuation in your net worth statement to be accurate to the dollar—you are just looking for sound estimates. It is not going to make much difference if you are a few hundred dollars out here and there.

If you are married or in a relationship which is more than short term, you will need to choose whether to do a joint worth statement or whether to consider your worth as if you were alone. Couples often have considerable joint assets like a family home, rental properties or a business—*but you need to consider what would be yours if you were to split up.* That can be quite a scary idea, but taking responsibility for your money includes considering the worst-case scenario. Considering what assets would be yours will usually mean splitting the value of most of your assets down the middle. Depending on your circumstances, your share could be more or less than half—some assets such as inheritances or property that is covered by a pre-nuptial agreement may not be jointly owned. It is very common for women to find that their individual net worth statement comes as a shock—what they would own if the relationship ceased would be very little and would mean a drastic change in lifestyle. A smart woman will ask herself whether she could survive on the assets that would be hers if her relationship ended. And could she thrive as well as survive?

Annie's and Bill's net worth statement looks like this:

| | | |
|---|---|---|
| *Assets* | | |
| *House* | *$480,000* | |
| *Rental property* | *$250,000* | |
| *Savings* | *$25,000* | |
| *Share portfolio (Bill's)* | *[$275,000]* | |
| | | *$755,000* |
| *Liabilities* | | |
| *Mortgage* | *$380,000* | |
| *Mortgage on rental property* | *$210,000* | |
| *Credit Card* | *$16,500* | |
| | | *$606,500* |
| *Net worth* | | *$148,500* |

*Annie and Bill have a joint net worth of $148,500. They have not been together all that long. Bill was very bitter about halving his assets when his marriage split up so he has tucked away his* *shares in a separate holding and they are not joint property. (Note that I did not add in Bill's shares, as these are held separately.) So Annie only has a net worth of half this total—$74,250. This is not very much given that she is in mid-life and has earned very well for decades. The other thing to note is that they would look very well off from the outside—a nice home (heavily mortgaged), a rental property (but only a small deposit has been paid), nice vehicles (but they don't own them) and a high level of credit card debt (they are living high and will be paying a lot of interest on this level of debt).*

The acid test is to work out what would be yours if you were to split tomorrow. When you have that number, you know your starting point and can start to think about what you need to do to establish a better financial footing. You cannot afford to ignore your financial position and you shouldn't proceed as if someone else will take care of the rest.

You should do a net worth statement often. It tells you how well off you are financially and it tells you whether you are trending in the right direction—that is, are you worth more or less? Your net worth will change as you make decisions to buy or sell things, and as your savings and investments grow. Your net worth statement tells you how well you are doing financially—and how financially independent you are. You will want to set annual goals for your net worth and then track them to see how well you are doing. Over time, you will want your net worth to increase. I would recommend that you do a net worth statement annually (and preferably every six months). If you graph your net worth over time, it will hopefully look like the graph on page 27.

One of the nicest lines in the world is a rising net worth graph! Doing a net worth statement often (including after any major change in circumstances) and adding your new position to the graph lets you see how you are doing at a glance. It gives you immediate feedback on the effect of your decisions and hopefully will show you that you are making progress in the right direction.

Net worth over a lifetime

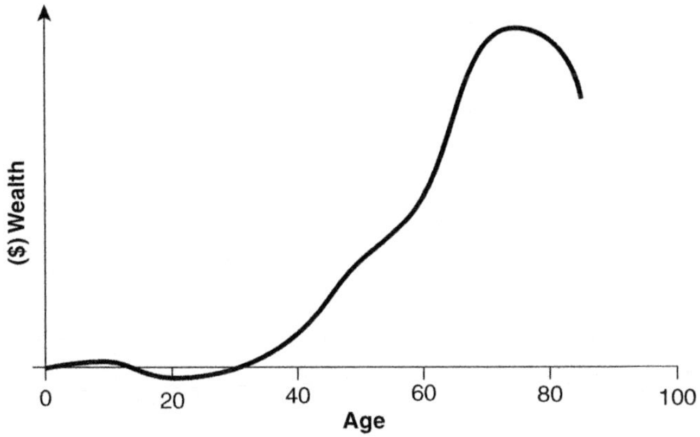


Net worth statements will make you very conscious of your financial position. Above all, they help you to distinguish clearly between lifestyle and *actual* wealth—it's all too easy to be living as if you were rich when in fact you are actually quite poor. You will begin to have an awareness of your financial position and you will start to think about decisions you make in terms of how they affect your net worth.

Net worth statements also let you examine where exactly your money is. Is your wealth tied up in 'good' assets which are growing in value and perhaps giving you income, or are your assets (such as your family home) providing no income and costing you lots of money to maintain? Property *has* grown a lot in value over the last couple of years, but this is unlikely to continue at the same rate. And your home is not a good place to have all your wealth locked away.

You will also scrutinise your liabilities more carefully. How much are those debts costing you? Not all debt is equal—you may start to notice, for example, how much your credit card debt is costing you each year and you may decide to make some better choices about how you manage your liabilities.

I think net worth statements are very valuable because they help you see the reality of your finances and they help you see the impact of the choices that you make. All the choices are still yours—but it's good to know what the longer term effects of the decisions we make every day are likely to be.

Your net worth statement tells you where you are today—your starting point. It is a snapshot of your position at any given time. Regularly compiling a net worth statement will tell you how you are doing on your path to financial independence.

## SMART WOMAN STRATEGIES

A smart woman would do a personal net worth statement. This involves:

- ♀ listing all the assets she owns (or 50 per cent of the value of those she *jointly* owns);
- ♀ listing all her liabilities (or 50 per cent of her *joint* liabilities such as the mortgage);
- ♀ subtracting the liabilities from the assets. This net worth number would be the sum of her personal wealth if it were all cashed up today.

# 6
# WHERE DOES YOUR MONEY COME FROM?

The other thing you really want to know is how much income you have each year. The easiest way to work this out is to do an *income statement*. Many women are very unclear about how much income they have each year, but it can be very simple to calculate if you are a wage or salary earner. Take your pay slip and figure out how much you get each year. You may have twelve (or thirteen) monthly payments each year, or 26 fortnightly payments, or 52 weekly payments. Tax has probably been deducted and if you have no other income the calculation is quite simple.

If you have income from rental property or from a trust, or if you receive dividends or money from any other source, gather up your statements and add up the income. You need to know what is coming in (in-come) each year. You can do this before or after tax—just make sure that you are consistent and that you don't mix amounts that are before tax with other amounts that have already had the tax paid.

Marnie's income statement is:

| | |
|---|---|
| Salary | $65,000 (after tax) |
| Rental income | $5,000 (after expenses and tax) |
| Total income | $70,000 (after tax) |

*Marnie has a very good job and her annual salary after she pays tax is $65,000. She also owns a rental property (still heavily indebted), but even after she has covered her expenses and paid tax it nets her an extra $5000. So her total annual income is $70,000.*

You can do your own income statement. The main headings you will need are:

*Salary/wage*
*Interest*
*Rental income*
*Dividends*
*Income from trust*
*Other*

## TOTAL ANNUAL INCOME

You probably have to collect all of this for a tax return every year anyway. It is very useful when you are starting to plan for your financial future to have a clear sense of where you are starting from—it will help you set reasonable goals and will show you which areas should get priority in your plans.

Many of the women I have worked with who are in relationships are often quite surprised when they confront the fact that they have little or no income. Withdrawing money from an ATM is not income—even if it seems relatively unlimited at the moment. The acid test is what your income would be if you were alone tomorrow.

Income matters. Even if your net worth statement shows that you are quite wealthy, it doesn't necessarily mean you have any income to live on. Women who own or jointly own a house may have a net worth of hundreds of thousands of dollars—but they can't eat that or pay bills with it. Women who have no income of their own are very vulnerable—even if they are living very well at present. If anything happens to their relationship (illness, death, trauma or divorce), they will need to find a source of income very quickly. Depending on their skills, how long they have been out of the workforce, where they live, and other responsibilities like children, this can be very difficult—especially in the short term. I meet a great many women who seem oblivious to the financial problems they might face without a secure source of income.

One of the other benefits of doing an income statement is that it makes you very conscious of how much money flows through your hands—even if you have convinced yourself that you are very poor.

Take a hypothetical situation. Let's say you earned $40,000 a year and that you worked over a lifetime for 40 years. (Now I know that no one earns the same each year but humour me for the sake of the figures.) $40,000 does not seem like a huge amount. But that adds up to $1,600,000—over one and a half million dollars in total. If you look at it like that, it's a lot. If I assured you that you would earn that amount, you would take money very seriously and you would do a plan for your finances. But we get our money in small lumps—weekly, fortnightly or monthly. We are often desperate for it to arrive and seem to gobble it up in no time. Because our heads are down in the detail of managing from payday to payday—and most women do a huge amount of juggling—we never realise the huge sums of money that we are managing. Doing an income statement is one way of helping you realise just how big the sums are.

Knowing your net worth and your income lets you begin to look at the big picture. Many women get very used to juggling from payday to payday—they are very practised at managing the micro detail of each week or month but never stop to look at the bigger picture of their overall finances. If you want to become financially independent, you have to move beyond the weekly or monthly pay period and start to think in terms of years and decades.

## SMART WOMAN STRATEGIES

A smart woman would do a personal income statement. This involves calculating:

- ♀ what kind of income she has—from paid work, rental property, dividends, trusts, etc.;
- ♀ how much income per year she has; and
- ♀ what the total income is before and after tax.

# 7
# YOUR MONEY HABITS

When you have done your net worth statement and an income statement, you will know your starting point. Think of these statements as giving you your global positioning system position on the Planet of Financial Independence.

The next step is to look at how you currently handle money—your *money habits*. Lots of people talk about money personalities, but I prefer to think of them as habits or behaviours. It's far harder to change your personality—after all, that is who you are.

But what you do with money is not *you*—it is just your behaviour, and you are free to choose to change your behaviour or habits any time you see fit. Some habits serve you well and you may want to keep them; others get in the way of your financial self-sufficiency.

So what kinds of money habits and behaviours do you have? When you have a choice, what do you usually do? And are these habits taking you in the direction of financial *dependence* or financial *independence*?

Take the **Money Habits Test**. Then add up your score. You can plot your score on the **Money Habits Meter.**

Money Habits Test

| Money habits I have | Always (Score 5) | Sometimes (Score 3) | Never (Score 0) |
|---|---|---|---|
| 1. I pay for everything (except a house) in cash. | | | |
| 2. I manage my mortgage actively. | | | |

| | | | |
|---|---|---|---|
| 3. I have money left over at the end of each pay period. | | | |
| 4. I know how much is in my accounts. | | | |
| 5. I have an emergency fund. | | | |
| 6. I know my net worth. | | | |
| 7. I have a savings plan. | | | |
| 8. I read articles and books on personal finance. | | | |
| 9. I talk about investments with family, friends and colleagues. | | | |
| 10. I have a long-term personal finance plan. | | | |
| 11. I have a written personal finance plan. | | | |
| 12. I make annual goals for my finances. | | | |
| 13. I have a personal budget. | | | |
| 14. I minimise personal expenses. | | | |
| 15. I know how much income I have each year. | | | |
| 16. I know how I am doing against budget at any time. | | | |
| 17. I keep receipts and claim all the expenses I can. | | | |
| 18. I have a retirement (super) plan. | | | |
| 19. I live within my means. | | | |
| 20. I read the business section in the newspaper. | | | |
| 21. I pay my credit card in full every month. | | | |
| 22. I budget for entertainment, hobbies, gifts, etc. | | | |
| 23. I plan carefully for big purchases. | | | |
| 24. I never have (non-tax deductible) debt except for my mortgage. | | | |

| | | |
|---|---|---|
| 25. I get expert help when I need it. | | |
| 26. I insure my house and other assets. | | |
| 27. I insure my income. | | |
| 28. I invest in my knowledge and skills. | | |
| 29. I ask for a pay rise every year. | | |
| 30. I change jobs if I can't get ahead. | | |
| 31. I organise my accounts to reduce bank fees. | | |
| 32. I have an up-to-date will. | | |
| 33. I have an Enduring Power of Attorney. | | |
| 34. I have all of my financial records in one place. | | |
| 35. I spend time every month on my finances. | | |
| 36. I use my own bank's ATM. | | |
| 37. I never incur late payment penalties. | | |
| 38. I take advantage of early payment incentives. | | |
| 39. I shop around for most items. | | |
| 40. I feel I am in charge of my finances. | | |
| 41. I wait to buy things until I have considered it carefully. | | |
| 42. I make savings through automatic payments. | | |
| 43. I explore opportunities to increase my income. | | |
| 44. I work to minimise tax. | | |
| 45. I take advantage of employee benefits. | | |
| 46. I pay my bills online to reduce fees. | | |
| 47. I withdraw enough cash to avoid EFTPOS charges. | | |

| | | | |
|---|---|---|---|
| 48. I save any bonuses I receive. | | | |
| 49. I reinvest interest I earn. | | | |
| 50. I never borrow for value-losing assets. | | | |
| TOTALS | | | |

Money Habits Meter

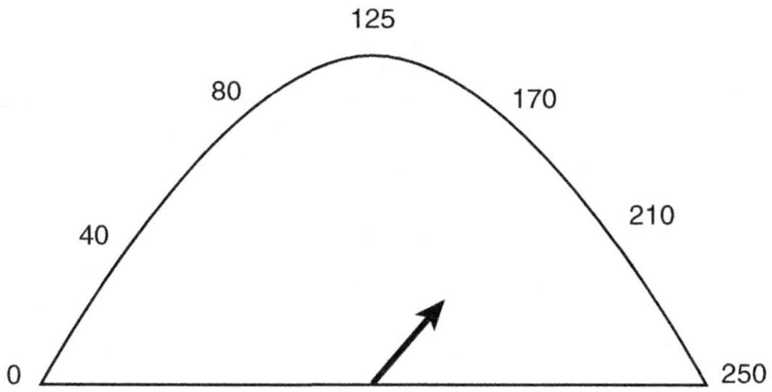


## UNDERSTANDING YOUR SCORE

All of the habits described in the test are good habits—they will take you in the direction of becoming self-sufficient and financially independent.

- ♀ *210+ You are motoring along!* Your habits are very good and you are doing most of the things you need to to ensure you become financially independent. Have a close look at the questions you did not score a 5 on—these will probably be the final touch to what is already a great performance. Congratulations! You should be writing this book—not reading it!
- ♀ *170+ You are doing well.* You must be doing most things right, at least some of the time. Ask yourself why you are not more consistent—you obviously know a lot about what you need

to do. Is your attitude stopping you? Is your partner or someone else derailing you? If you did a bit more of the right stuff consistently your performance would rocket up.

- ♀ *125+ Well, you can't plead ignorance!* You either have some good habits because you picked them up along the way (perhaps your family provided a good model for managing money?) or you are in the process of changing your ways but have not quite got there yet. Examine the statements you scored poorly on and pick a few that you feel you can change immediately. You'll be so delighted with the difference in your money performance that you'll be hooked and back for more before long.
- ♀ *80+ You either don't care very much about your money or you don't yet know what you need to be doing.* It must be the latter or you wouldn't be doing this test. You need to start doing the habits on this list ASAP. Read on for a better understanding of why these will work for you.
- ♀ *40+ Your finances must be in a sad state.* The only way from here is up. Do yourself a favour—take a day off and read the whole book. Take five of these habits this week and start doing them. Then take another five . . . You will never be free and independent if you do not take action to change your habits—but the good news is that, if you do adopt these habits, you will be in charge of your money and your future.
- ♀ *0–39. This is a Disaster Zone.* There is one bright spot—you are reading about the management of your money. Remember anyone can manage money—and do it well. Read on. Small changes will make a very big difference if you stick at it. Be a late bloomer.

## SMART WOMAN STRATEGIES

A smart woman would look at her money habits and:

- ♀ start doing the ones she's never done;
- ♀ do the ones she sometimes does more often; and
- ♀ keep doing the ones she always does.

# 8
# WHAT ARE YOU DOING WITH YOUR MONEY NOW?

By now, you should have an idea of what it will take for you to be financially independent—that is, able to provide the means for yourself to live in a way that you find reasonable and comfortable.

Now is the time to take a good look at what you are currently doing with your money every week and month. You have already completed a net worth statement and done the sums to see what annual income you have. The women I work with often find these exercises quite shocking. They often say things like 'I can't believe I have this amount of income and yet I never have any money' or 'I have been earning well for years and yet I have nothing to show for it' or 'Given how much income I have, why don't I seem to be able to be or do or have any of these things I say I want in my life?'

It can be a shock to realise the truth when we finally write down the figures and look at them. Perhaps it's because we secretly know we are not going to like what we see that we avoid doing these sums for so long!

You may also have been shocked at your money habits test score—and have already resolved to do better. Don't beat yourself up—remember that most of us learned all of the wrong things about money management as we grew up. Those habits can be changed.

But there may be another shock on the way when you start tracking what is happening to your income. Business calls this an audit—but it simply means tracking (on paper) where every cent is going. Remember, those small amounts that we often ignore or forget about could be funding all those things that you would like to be, have and do.

Many of the women I have worked with find that the easiest way to do this is to carry a small notebook around for a few weeks or months and note every expenditure—including parking money, ice-creams for the kids when you get petrol, cups of coffee, bus fares, and so on.

When you have enough information you can add the sums up under various headings. We all find it easy to remember that we pay hundreds of dollars for power, phone calls and petrol—but, depending on our habits, we can get huge surprises in some of the other categories. Many women are very surprised at the totals under drycleaning, cosmetics, lunches, takeaways, magazines, parking, coffee, etc. A client often finds that there is already enough being spent on stuff that she doesn't care about very much (such as lunch) to fund something that she really does care about and thought was out of the question (such as travel, mortgage or share investments).

You can collect your spending information under however many categories you like. If you use a smaller number, it will be more manageable—but you may miss some critical information.

*Eleanor, for example, found she was spending $300 a week at the supermarket. It was only when she broke this spending into further categories that she realised nearly $70 of that was going on hot takeaway food on the evenings she shopped.*

Likewise, it's easy to miss what you are *really* doing at the service station—the $50 worth of petrol may end up being $75 after each fill when you add on the cigarettes, ice-creams, papers and even groceries.

A suggested shortlist of categories would include majors like:

*rent or mortgage;*
*utilities (like electricity and water);*
*transport (car, bus);*
*food;*
*clothes;*
*entertainment (hobbies, outings, sport);*

*gifts (birthdays, charity);*
*medical/dental; and*
*miscellaneous.*

It is probably best to keep this list quite simple to start with. If you find that a category seems to contain a lot of expenditure or items, then you might want to break it down further.

'Miscellaneous' might include frightening levels of expenditure under such sub-headings as:

*laundry;*
*drycleaning;*
*coffee;*
*lunches;*
*cigarettes;*
*chocolate;*
*treats for kids;*
*ice-creams;*
*school lunch money;*
*takeaways;*
*cosmetics;*
*flowers;*
*greeting cards;*
*babysitting;*
*eating out;*
*manicures;*
*hairdresser.*

Many of these categories will be all too familiar. You can file these expenses under any of the above headings you like, but make sure you don't lose sight of them—they may well be consuming all the money that could potentially make you financially independent.

*One woman I worked with had a huge amount listed under 'Medical'. When I inquired with great sympathy and concern for her health I discovered that she was fighting fit but had hidden all of the impulse purchases at the cosmetics counter, the beauty treatments, the acrylic nails and the hairdresser's costs in that category. It had looked like she was funding a private hospital!*

So it's really up to you. Above all else, you don't want to fool *yourself* on this. It's your money and you can spend it however you like. But you can't choose to do anything else with it until you know where it is going now. Resolve to find out exactly where and how you are spending your money.

Some women like to use a small diary to track their spending. It can be very interesting to see what the *patterns* of spending are over the week—for example, you might spend without thinking on Friday nights after a drink or two or you may be very vulnerable to impulse spending when you are tired or rushing home after work. Just like breaking a diet, our spending is often triggered by different things. Many people overspend on groceries when they are hungry; others get carried away when they go for an after-work drink and end up spending big on dinner out and a taxi home. Working late can be another trigger: you're tired and feel you should be rewarded, or you may feel guilty because you're late home and so treat the kids. Again, all of these are your choices; however, it does help to be aware of what you do and what events, timing, or feelings trigger your spending. It may help you to note the day, the time and even how you were feeling when you made purchases—especially if you feel your spending is getting away on you. And if you spend all your income every pay period, or if you have debt on your credit card, then your spending *is* out of control.

You can do your analysis of what you find with a friend—you will probably both laugh and cry! Ask yourself whether this is how you wish to spend your income. Is your spending serving you or enslaving you? Are you trapped in this pattern and therefore preventing yourself from ever having the money to fund all those other things you feel are important? You will find yourself starting to reallocate your income in your head. Some of your categories can be eliminated altogether if you wish (for example, lunches or magazines), whereas others can be reduced (such as telephone and electricity or entertainment).

'Budget' is a word that strikes fear in the heart of the strongest woman, but it is only a plan. And it's *your* plan for *your* money—not something imposed by anyone else. Once you have a good sense of where your money is going now, you can start to plan/budget for where it will go from now on so that you can fund the things that you have decided you want in your life.

There will be some basic choices here:

- You might decide that your current income is insufficient to allow you to live what you consider to be a reasonable life. If that is the case, you will need to put some energy and effort into growing your income so that it can fund your plan for financial independence.
- You might decide that you don't want to make the effort required to fund some of the things you want. Working less, rather than more, may be very important to you. In that case, you should revise your expectations so that your income can cover them, being careful to make sure that the non-negotiables like accommodation are still taken care of. You can choose to take out some of the extras—discretionary spending or negotiables—and still be independent on quite a low income.
- Your timeline may need adjusting. Often it is quite possible to fund everything you want—but not right *now*. You might, for example, find that owning your home will take most of your effort for years, and that art lessons, travel or other investments may have to be given a due date several years hence.

> Your goal is to be financially self-sufficient and independent—able to meet your own needs on your own income for as long as you live.

## SMART WOMAN STRATEGIES

A smart woman would find out exactly where her money goes:

- ♀ She would buy a notebook to track where every cent of her money is going.
- ♀ When she has enough data (several weeks or months), she would add the expenditure up under different categories.
- ♀ She would look at each category and ask herself whether she wants to spend so much of her income in that area. How much could she 'save' in that area so she could spend it on things she considers to be more important?

# 9
# YOUR MONEY LIFELINE

Every woman is unique, but the patterns of our lives have many similarities. The place and role of money in our lives will also follow certain trends.

If you graph the amount of net worth that women have on average, the picture will look something like this:

A Woman's Money Lifeline

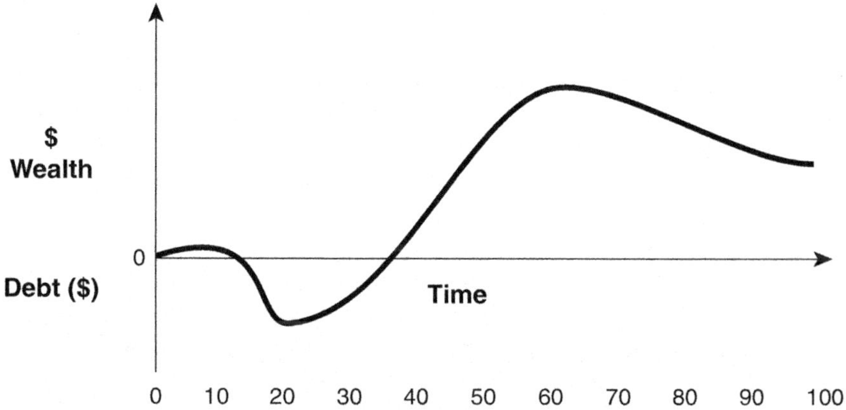


It works like this: In our early years we have little or no money. We might have some pocket money or an after-school job during our teens. There might be a little money against our name in a bank account or a trust somewhere—our parents or grandparents may have made a gift or deposit.

Typically we will have negative net worth in our late teens. This is especially true nowadays as young people borrow for student loans. The graph dips below the line.

As we start work, we begin to pay off the loan and accumulate savings. We may feel very hard pressed for money if we have bought a house, but typically—even though we are short of cash—our net worth is rising. How high it goes will depend on how well we are earning and how well we are spending—some people stay in negative net worth (they *owe* more than they own) while others manage their money well and accumulate savings. As careers progress and incomes rise, some people never get ahead—because they continue to spend everything that they earn. They may have a very high standard of living but if they cashed everything up they would be left with almost nothing by the time all the borrowings had been paid for. Others who may have had only a modest income will have managed it well and made good investments so that their net worth has continued to grow.

Typically, a woman's net worth will be at its highest around the beginning of retirement. This represents the wealth that has been created over a lifetime of earning, saving and investing. As women move into their later decades, net worth begins to drop as they spend more than they make in income. This is not always the case—income from investments may more than cover what they need to spend in order to live, and so the net worth graph continues to rise. Others may get a windfall from an inheritance and find themselves with quite a lot of money that they did not expect.

Ideally, in order to be assured of financial independence for your whole life, you want to get your net worth as high as you can before you need to start using it up to live on. The longer you can continue to grow it, and the higher the graph is at its peak, the more financially fit and financially independent you will be.

Lifelines will vary, of course. If you do extended study you may be in negative net worth until you are in your thirties. Financial disasters such as divorce or redundancy can cause your money lifeline to plateau or even dip sharply. Lifelines that go wrong through some disaster look like the graph on page 45. The effect of the disastrous event (redundancy, divorce, etc.) is that net worth is reduced and, for whatever reason, is very difficult to build again.

Money Lifeline Showing Effect of Disaster

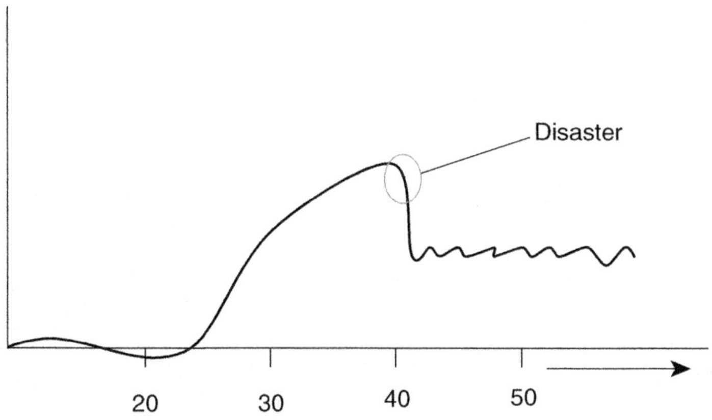


But the principle remains the same: you want the graph to climb as high as it can for as long as it can. And, ultimately, you want to be gone before the graph goes into the negative—that's what making your money last as long as you do really means!

Women typically have a succession of life stages: student with little or no money; twenty-something with independent earnings; thirty-something with relationships, marriages, children, mortgages, tight budgets, periods away from work, failed relationships; forty-something, returned to work part- or full-time, children growing up, new relationships, renewed careers; fifty-something with ageing parents, student children; sixty-something, retiring, second careers, retired partners, dependent parents, grandparent responsibilities. Everyone's pattern is slightly different but some of the stages are statistically predictable. All of them impact on a woman's finances. All of them need to be managed well if your goal is to be financially independent for the whole of your life.

It is your choice to manage these stages as you wish, but a smart woman would consider the impact of each choice on her money lifeline and take whatever steps she needed to still meet her goal of financial independence. If we put the typical life stages into table form, they would look something like this:

| Age | Activity | Financial concerns | Suggested priorities |
|---|---|---|---|
| 20–25 | • End of study<br>• First job<br>• Early independence | Personal spending on fun | • Repay any student debt<br>• Start a savings program, even if the amounts are very small<br>• Buy a house |
| 25–30 | • Relationships<br>• Growing career | • Mortgage<br>• Home expenses | • Joint account<br>• Life insurance<br>• Mortgage repayments as fast as possible |
| 30–40 | • Children<br>• Time out of the workforce<br>• Part-time work; return to work | • Mortgage<br>• Family expenses<br>• One income | • Mortgage repayments as fast as possible<br>• Other investments if possible<br>• Family protection, including insurances |
| 40–50 | • Full-time work again<br>• Teenagers | • Expensive teenagers<br>• Tertiary fees<br>• Retirement funds | • Pay off last of mortgage<br>• Diversified investments<br>• Protection of assets, e.g., family trust |
| 50+ | • Empty nest<br>• Retired<br>• Widowed? | • Retirement funds<br>• Inheritance | • Income-producing investments<br>• Selling down assets |

This life-stages table is very generic: every woman's pattern will be different depending on how she chooses to live her life. However, it is useful to think about roughly what stage you are at, what the main financial concerns you have at this stage are, and what your financial priorities ought to be. It helps to look ahead: what stage are you likely to be in next and what do you need to prepare for financially?

You can use the stages above together with the idea of a money lifeline to both plan to grow your net worth and plan what major financial activities happen in which period.

Emily's plan looks like this:

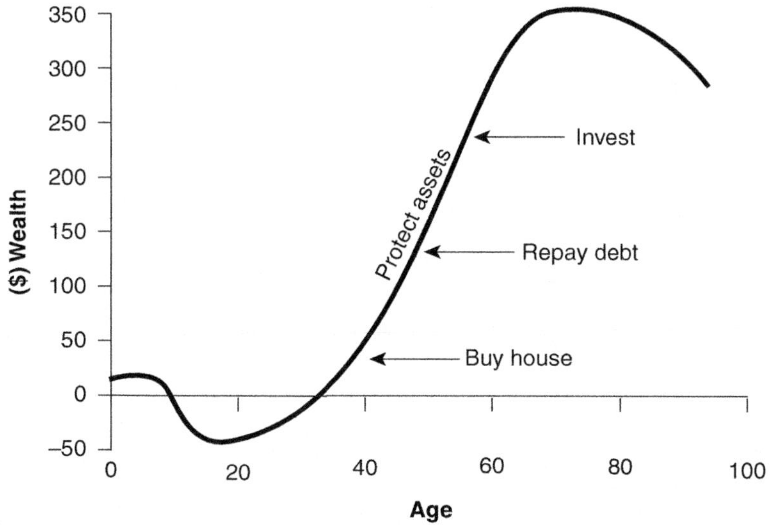


*Emily is committed to developing her net worth throughout her life so that she has good funding along the way and for her later years. She's 28 and the graph shows that she's almost finished repaying her student debt. Her plan is to buy her first house soon—just as quickly as she can save for a deposit. Her parents have promised that, if she can save $25,000, they will lend her $15,000 for the deposit. Even though that will mean taking on a huge mortgage, her net worth will begin to climb along with the value of her house. Sensibly, she plans a rigorous program of repaying the mortgage as fast as she can. She will then direct her savings, and hopefully all of the additional income she will be earning, into other investments. She plans a great life along the way—it won't be just mortgage repayments. But the important thing is that her money lifeline will continue to rise right into her later years.*

It is very easy to make life decisions that impact enormously on your financial position without being aware of the steps you are taking. No one rings a bell and warns you that something you are about to do may have dramatic effects on your finances for life!

It pays to be aware of the effect of your choices on your financial prospects. That way you will choose in awareness rather than mindlessly, and you can also take steps to secure your financial position at the same time.

> Money should never dictate how you choose to live your life.

Having a baby is a very good example. Along with great joy comes a lot of expense, and perhaps the cessation of paid work for a while. If you think about that in advance hopefully you will still decide to have the baby! But you might also consider living on one (or a much more constrained) income for the prior six months and you might also think about what you can do to keep earning while at home or how to keep your skills current for the period you will be out of work. You might also consider insuring your partner at a higher level for loss of life or loss of income. In addition, you might want to renegotiate mortgage repayments or the arrangements of your personal and joint accounts. Will you, for example, have any 'personal' money while you are off work?

Remember, you are trying to get your net worth as high as you can while still doing all of the things you want to do in your life. Small differences in how you handle money will make a huge difference over your total lifeline. On the next page is a template for you to draw your own money lifeline.

## SMART WOMAN STRATEGIES

A smart woman would understand where she was on the money lifeline and take action to decide where she needed to be:

- ♀ She would draw her own money lifeline to date. It does not need to be accurate to the dollar—it is just important to get a picture of the general trend.
- ♀ She would continue with a dotted line for the future, to predict what might happen if she continued as she was.
- ♀ She would then draw another dotted line (in a different colour) to show the money lifeline she wished to have in the future.
- ♀ She would think about what she would have to change to get her desired money lifeline.

Your Money Lifeline

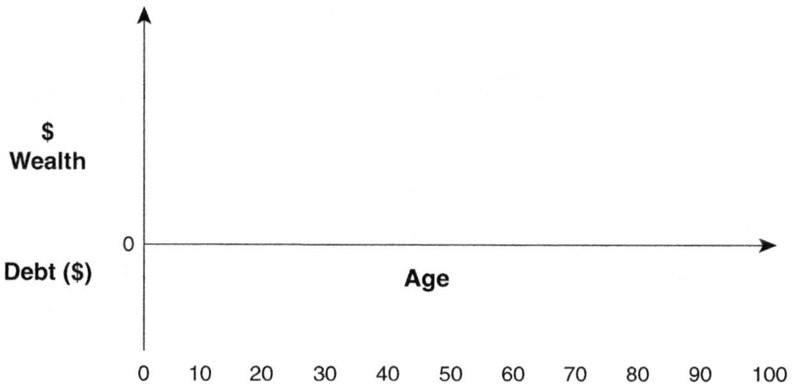

# PART III

# WORKING OUT WHAT YOU WANT

# 10
# A GIRL'S GOTTA DREAM!

*Money isn't important*. You don't expect to find a statement like that in a book about money. But it isn't really money that's important; it's the life it can create for you. Money is only a tool for helping you to achieve the life of your dreams. Most smart women aren't dreaming of untold riches, multiple homes, endless travel and a life of leisure—pleasant though all that would be. Most of us would be more than happy to have the basics taken care of, to be relatively worry-free and to have enough to indulge in a few of the pursuits that add spice, interest and meaning to our lives.

You can have a much bigger and better life if you can make yourself financially self-sufficient and can ensure financial independence right through to old age. Finance will largely dictate many of your choices—further education, career options, childcare, where and how you live, what you get to do and become.

The question you need to ask is what you *really* want from your life—and the earlier you ask it, the better. Of course, you can—and you will—change your mind on aspects of your ideal life from time to time. But at any given time, you have to decide what your values are and what is meaningful for you. Only then will you know what you want the money for, how much you will need, and how best to achieve your dream.

> What do you need money for? To live the life that you want to—the life you really want to live.

But don't start with money, start with *you*. Be warned—this is often the hardest part of taking charge of your life: you have to really think about what matters to you, what you are willing to insist on and what you will decide is unnecessary. We are not used to doing this kind of work on ourselves—it is far easier to fill our time dashing around meeting everyone's expectations other than our own.

Our consumer society encourages us to want and desire things on a whim. It tempts us with images of goods and services which are slickly presented and designed to make us feel that we are missing out if we don't have them. We rarely take the time to ask ourselves what kind of life we want for ourselves, what sort of lifestyle we would design beyond a shopping list of goods and thrills. It can take a lot of time and soul-searching to truly figure out what matters to us. Of course, we can't have, do and be everything, so we must choose. We probably *can* have the life we want as long as we are prepared to give up other things to have that life. That can feel quite frightening, especially if you have never even taken the time to clarify what it is that your heart truly desires.

Money is only useful if it can give you more of what you want and less of what you want to avoid. But you have to know what you want.

In the end, this process is about values. And clearly there are trade-offs—the more you insist on having or doing or being, the more you will have to work and sacrifice to make it happen. Having a lot is important to some people—and not very important at all to others. You will have financial independence when you have enough to take care of the things that are really important for *you*. It is easy to frighten people into thinking that they need hundreds of thousands of dollars just to survive retirement, but it ultimately comes down to you deciding what is essential for you.

If you don't take the time to think through what is really important to you, other people will try to do it for you. Family, friends and society will try to tell you what you must have, do and be. There is a huge marketing industry out there spending billions of dollars every day to convince you that you must have, do and be whatever it is that they are selling. The only way to withstand all of this pressure is to be clear about what you want for you. Don't let anyone else make these choices.

It is challenging to change our attitudes and habits and to apply the discipline we need to create financial freedom and independence. But it becomes much easier when we have a clear picture of what it is we are trying to create. So a smart woman will take the time and care to ask herself what she really wants. She will continue to ask that question regularly and to make sure that she has a very clear dream or vision about the life for which she is creating financial independence.

If we are committed to something that really matters to us, it is easy to put our money to work in that direction. We will find it much easier to make choices in line with our dream and we will be able to find the inspiration and the discipline to get what we truly want. It will feel like it's worth it!

It is very difficult to find the energy to begin to make changes and very hard to summon up the discipline to keep going if you are not clear about *why* you are doing it all. Vague notions about what's important to you will not be enough to keep you going when the going gets tough—and making changes *can* be tough. A clear sense of what is important to you and what matters in your life will give you a very strong motivation—to do the things you need to do to ensure your financial independence.

So a smart woman does lots of daydreaming. She constantly asks herself about what really matters. She makes sure that she knows herself well enough to choose what will make her really happy. A smart woman uses all of her senses to visualise herself being, doing, having whatever is important to her. You will never attain whatever you cannot visualise yourself being or doing. A smart woman helps herself by seeking out images that appeal—in books, movies, magazines and songs. So script the movie of the life you want or compose the song you want to sing—it is far too important to let anyone else do it for you.

> Deep down, women know what they really want, what stuff really matters and what is just gloss.

## SMART WOMAN STRATEGIES

A smart woman would spend some time dreaming about the rest of her life:

- ♀ She would dream a little and give herself the time and respect to consider what is really important to her.
- ♀ She would spend lots of time thinking about what is really, *really* important to her. She would think about her 'bottom line'—the minimum she is willing to settle for or put up with in the various areas of her life.
- ♀ She would get as clear a picture of her dreams and values as she could, using all her senses: drawing or painting pictures; creating a collage or scrapbook of images; selecting music that conveys her dream, and so on.
- ♀ She would write down her thoughts and list her goals, keeping them somewhere safe and returning to them often.

# 11
# THE PRACTICAL ART OF DREAMING

It is important not to plan your financial strategy until you are very clear about what you want in your life. It often helps to jot down some of your thoughts and ideas at this point—perhaps with the help of a friend or partner.

Imagine that you are living your ideal life some time in the future (in five, ten or fifteen years, for example).

> *Where would you be?*
> *What would you be doing?*
> *What is each day like for you?*
> *Who is in your 'family'?*
> *How would others describe you now?*
> *How do you feel?*

You don't have to do all of this in words. Some women find that they prefer to draw—big sheets of paper and thick crayons or felt-tip pens work best. Others find that music is their best medium—they find snatches of sound and lyrics that really speak about what matters to them. Often the most successful approach is to begin with a collage—to find images that really appeal to you from magazines and paste them up on a huge sheet of paper to represent what is important to you. You can keep adding new images as they catch your eye.

This may seem like just a bit of fun, but it's actually one of the most important steps you can take on the road to financial independence. The underlying questions you are answering are:

*What is it that the real you yearns for?*
*How do you want to live?*
*What do you care most about?*
*What kind of person do you want to become?*
*How do you want to feel and what would have to happen for you to feel that way most of the time?*

These are all questions about what you value, about what motivates and drives you. They are really important questions in every woman's life but we are often discouraged from asking them; rather, we are encouraged to think short-term or to do what suits others in our lives. More than ever before in history, we now have both the freedom to ask these questions and the means to act on the answers—will you rise to the challenge?

Stop and think for a while. What are the absolutely 'must haves' for you? What do you want to acquire?

Perhaps it is a secure income? A house? Enough money to ensure your child's safety and well-being? A reliable car?

*Rachel really wants to buy a house within the next year. She is determined to have it paid off in a decade—before her fortieth birthday. She is insistent that both her children will have a secure family home. Rachel says she will do whatever it takes to make this happen for her kids. She grew up in a sole-parent household too, and she always swore that her kids would never have to keep flat-hopping the way she and her mum did.*

What will be the 'must do' things in your life? What do you want to achieve? Being able to visit family every year? Enough leisure for daily exercise? An overseas trip?

*Sandra has two absolute 'must dos'. She is committed to being the first person in her family to get a degree. This is pretty ambitious, as she didn't finish high school. However, she has been doing really well at work and has enrolled in a top-up program at the local high school. Her manager has indicated that, if she continues to do well, the company might consider subsidising her further studies. If you met her, you'd believe she is serious. Her second 'must do' is that she wants to go trekking in Tibet. She's not sure why, but she has always been fascinated by that part of the world.*

Who do you want to be? Who do you wish to become? A loving partner in a great relationship? An at-home mum until your child has finished primary school? An artist? A reader?

*Clare's dream is to be retired in ten years' time so that she can be a full-time volunteer at the street kids' refuge. She has a passion to contribute and be of service. She already does a lot of voluntary work, but her full-time job limits her participation. She knows she has great managerial and counselling skills to offer and believes that this is the path which will add true meaning to her life.*

The purpose of these questions is to provoke you to think about your bottom line and how much money you will need to achieve what you want—what it is that you are going to insist on having, doing and being so that life will be good for you. Even if you cannot have everything you would like on the menu, at least be clear about what is absolutely fundamental and essential for your own well-being—and then work out how to make it happen. But it all starts with being clear about the life you want. The money comes second—you only need it to get what you have decided is the bottom line for you. It's being clear and really committed to your 'must be', 'must have' and 'must do' goals that will give you the motivation and the energy to make them happen. Vague wishes about the future don't activate people; clear pictures of what you'll be doing, what'll you'll have and who you'll be *will*.

Another approach to thinking about what matters to you is to look at different aspects of your life and decide what you want in each of them. It is easy to think of this as a life pie.

Life Pie

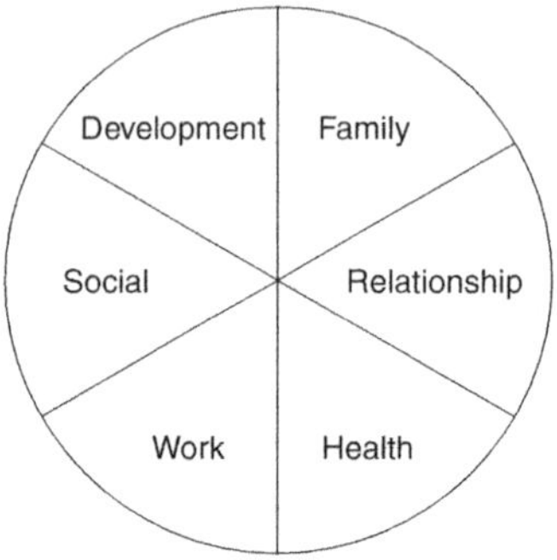


You might, for example, ask yourself what you want to have in your:

- ♀ family life (time together, visits, special occasions, creating great memories);
- ♀ relationship (intimacy, time together, shared dreams and activities);
- ♀ work (income, security, achievement, promotion, authority);
- ♀ health (fitness, weight control, exercise, sport, non-smoking);
- ♀ social life (friendship, fun, outings);
- ♀ development (personal growth, learning, being skilled at something of your choice.

What would make you feel that you had what you needed in each of these areas (or others of your choice)?

*Diane says that, even though she and her partner have a happy family life, she really wants to take the whole family on a tour of Australia before they all grow up and start to leave home (or refuse to go on family holidays!). This has some urgency, as her eldest is fifteen. However, it is really important to her and it would mean that both she and Trevor would have to arrange leave without pay at work as well as forgoing income for several months.*

*She wants to work on their relationship too—she feels that they have learned to ignore each other as they have been busy working and bringing up three kids for the last fifteen years. She feels that she could do this by converting one of the bedrooms into a small sitting room that would be off limits to the kids—somewhere for the parents to talk and have some peace and quiet.*

*Diane is not interested in her paid work except as a source of very necessary income. However, she is determined to continue to work and to earn even more—there are all the extras to pay for with the kids and she wants a surplus to save and invest for retirement. Her company is installing a call centre and she wants to do whatever is necessary to get a supervisory role that would pay about 20 per cent more than she currently earns.*

*Not surprisingly, Diane's own well-being—especially her weight and fitness levels—has been neglected in her busy life. Her ideal future would include her being a fit, energetic and active person who could enjoy her family for decades to come. She feels she could combine this dream with some more social life for her—some of her friends have organised a wellness group that arranges walks, treks, tennis, swimming and other outings.*

These are all ways to access what is really important to you. But you also need to look at the other side of the coin: what will you really regret *not* having, doing or being? What things would have to change in which areas of your life for you to feel that life was the way you wanted it to be? The clearer the image you have of what you want, the easier it is to take steps in that direction and to make the necessary changes.

It also pays to keep asking yourself *why* something is important to you. This is a search for the underlying value. It is important to me to travel to Ireland each year. Why? To see my family (huge and ever growing!). Why? Because their well-being and security are really important. As much as possible, you want to get to the core of what matters to you. That often opens up other ways of meeting that same value in your life.

It is common for the women I work with to begin with a long list of stuff they want to have and do and be. When they ask themselves lots of 'why' questions about this list, they usually find that behind the list are things they deeply want in their lives, such as:

*peace of mind;*
*security;*
*affection;*
*friendship;*
*family and friends;*
*making a contribution;*
*learning;*
*time for others;*
*self-esteem;*
*respect;*
*expertise;*
*wealth;*
*love;*
*pleasure;*
*fun;*
*independence;*
*service; and*
*leadership.*

Most people find that there are only a few values that really matter to them. If you have pages of values, you are unlikely to be very committed to any of them. This is mostly an exercise about clarifying what is on your short-list. It can be a good idea to make yourself choose only three to five values.

Some women may prefer to think about all of these things in private—it can be very threatening to share what is really in your heart about these matters. Others will find it easier to work through these questions with a partner or friend—but do choose someone who really cares about you, who won't pour scorn on what matters to you.

Write down your thoughts, reflections and insights. There is nothing like capturing things on paper and you will want to come back to this over and over again. Once you start thinking about what you really value in life, you will never stop. And this is what money and financial independence are for: to make sure that the things that you value can be made to happen and be protected.

> If you don't know what matters to you no amount of money will ever be enough!

The detail of your dream is important only to you. The dream will give you the energy to make the changes that you need to. You can be clever with money without having any life dreams or goals—but that's not always smart.

## SMART WOMAN STRATEGIES

A smart woman would spend even *more* time dreaming about the rest of her life:

- ♀ She would consider her values, choosing the three to five values most important to her. She would need to be as clear as possible about her values so that she could plan to meet their needs.
- ♀ Then she would think about some of the things she wants to have, do and be over and above the minimum. These are the bits that add spice and meaning to life.
- ♀ She would limit the list—if everything is important to her then nothing *really* is. She needs to ask herself whether each value is important enough to give up other things for.

# 12
# THE SERIOUS BUSINESS OF THE REST OF YOUR LIFE

As you clarify your dreams and values, a picture of the life you are choosing to live will start to emerge. Many women find it useful to think of the various aspects of their lives as 'businesses' that they are going to run. All women are familiar with having to fill lots of roles: daughter, mother, sister, friend, lover, colleague, worker, boss. One of the advantages of thinking about aspects of your life as a group of 'businesses' or 'projects' is that it is easier to take them seriously.

I frequently coach women who can talk very eloquently about all of the things that are important to them; often, however, the only aspect—or 'business'—in their lives that they really pay attention to (that is, fund with time, energy and money) is their paid work and career. Seeing *all* of the strands of your life as 'businesses' helps you to take them seriously in your own mind.

So what businesses do you want to fund in your life? If you know what you want, it is easy to work out how much you need to fund it. Then you can get busy on finding that money as creatively as you can. Even more importantly, you will know what aspects of life you are no longer prepared to fund. And that will help you free up money (as well as time and energy) to reallocate to projects that matter to you.

The whole point of all this deliberation is to work out what amount of money you would need to live in a satisfying way if you funded it all yourself. What does it cost to live in the way you wish?

*In planning for several of the businesses in her life, Janine has chosen to use the life pie headings as her framework. You can see from her plan that she has become clearer about the detail of what she wants—and has used the idea of 'business investment' to estimate what each aspect will cost her in terms of time, money or energy.*

*She has also chosen to name each of her businesses with a character—for example, 'Family Frieda' is her name for the business that takes care of her family and her life at home. Janine is singling out each of these businesses as things that are really important to her. She is clear about the values that each business meets. Her Family Frieda business, for example, meets her values of security, independence and joy.*

*She is quite clear about the things she wants to happen in each of her life businesses—in her Family Frieda business, for instance, she is determined to own a home for the family, to have time to spend with her child, to be able to see her overseas family and to create a wonderful home garden.*

*Janine has also worked through how much she will have to invest—that is, what it will cost her—in these projects to make these things happen in her life. The end result is that she really knows what she wants and the funds she will need.*

| Projects in my life | Values I am meeting | Things I want to do | Business investment—time/energy/money |
|---|---|---|---|
| **'Family Frieda'**<br>The project of taking care of my family, including home life | Security<br>Independence<br>Joy | Own a home<br>Have time at home with child<br>Paid childcare when needed<br>Visiting family overseas<br>Create lovely garden<br>Take care of ill parent | $40,000 for house deposit<br>Enough savings to work part-time/pay for childcare<br>$2,000 p.a. for family visits<br>$10,000 to create garden<br>$$$/time for parent |

| | | | |
|---|---|---|---|
| **'Social Sally'** *The project of fun, friends and social life* | *Friendship* *Fun* | *See friends regularly* *Outings to movies or meals* | *Afford a babysitter* *$50 per week for outings* |
| **'Learning Lisa'** *The business of self-development and lifelong growth* | *Self-esteem* *Independence* | *Continue to study for diploma* *Read widely* *Courses in areas of interest* | *$1,000 p.a. for study* *$100 per month for books/courses* *One hour a day for study* *Saturday mornings for assignments* |
| **'Alive Alicia'** *The business of health and wellness* | *Wellness* *Fun* | *Daily activity* *Bushwalking trips (family?)* *Get organised—so sleep, eat and exercise well* | *Time each day (childcare?)* *Day hike every month* *$500 of gear each year* *Better routines for family* |
| **'Marketing Marjorie'** *The business of work and career* | *Achievement* *Respect* *Independence* *Security* | *Finish qualification* *Get promotion* *Get a raise every year* *Get on leadership course at work* | *$1,000 p.a. for study (as above)* *Read about negotiation* *Prepare case for raise* |
| **'Contributing Charlotte'** *The business of meaning and spirituality* | *Contribution* *Achievement* | *Provide help at local home for elderly* | *One day a month* |

Once you have a good sense of what's important in your life, it is much easier to get into the planning for what exactly that would mean in practice and what amounts of money you will need to devote to meeting these values.

Have a look through your written notes and identify the top five or six areas you want to focus on. Frequently, the same values—independence or security—will keep emerging in your notes. You might then ask yourself what you want to focus on or make happen in order to meet these needs or desires. Depending on your individual circumstances, you might then choose to focus on owning your own home or getting the skills for a secure job as practical things you can do in order to meet your needs and values.

Examples of values in practical terms include:

> ***Independence****—get a qualification that leads to secure work;*
> ***Security*** *for children—own my home;*
> ***Family****—earn enough to afford good childcare/work part-time; save enough to afford to stop work for two years when a baby arrives.*

As you continue with this process, you will get more and more specific. It is very hard to take action on vague or imprecise goals. The clearer you can be about what you want or need to do to get to your desired level of financial independence, the easier it will be to go on to the next stage. The idea is to get to the point where it is clear what you are going to do tomorrow, and every day from then on, to get what you need and want in your life.

So continue to ask yourself questions—for example, if you wanted to own your own home:

> *What value would it be?*
> *Where would it be?*
> *When would you have found it?*
> *How much of a deposit would you want?*

A friend or partner can help you with this and can push you to be as specific as possible—the more vivid the picture you are creating in your head, the easier it will be to take action.

Keep writing everything down. Where possible, put numbers in as well—if you need a $350,000 house, that is quite different to wanting one costing $200,000 or $500,000. You can't plan properly around 'sort of' or vague ideas about what you want.

You are going to be working and saving for the life you are describing (rather than just working for a living), so make it as clear and important to you as possible. If all this book does is get you excited enough about some of your dreams and values to take action, then that will be more than enough. Some of these matters that you are choosing to make important won't cost you any money, but others will. Smart women get these things down on paper—they start to look real and you start to believe that they are really going to happen.

A smart woman once said she wouldn't invest in anything that she couldn't draw with a crayon—in other words, it needed to be a clear simple picture. You will be investing your life in what you are planning here. Can you draw yourself a picture of what you want? Go ahead—it's a great exercise. These drawings will inspire you forever.

As you cost each of your planned goals, inspire yourself further by writing yourself a cheque for the cost of each one. This is fun, even if you have no money in your account—this is a cheque from you for your heart's desire. Many of these cheques will need to be postdated by several years—you will not want, or may not be able, to take action on all your desired projects at once.

This relates to the money lifeline—you may want to promise yourself that the $10,000 you need for a certain project will be available to cash that cheque in 2010 when you will be 42. You might, for example, write a post-dated cheque to Thomas Cook Travel for $15,000 for a mid-life overseas trip to Europe. Dates and ages and 'cheques' to yourself are all ways of making these plans as real and as credible as possible. It's a way of promising yourself that you will do what it takes to realise your goals.

> If you don't know what financial independence means for you then all you end up doing is plucking numbers out of the air.

Many women value ongoing security highly. In practical terms, this will translate into owning a home or having enough income to keep pace with rental rises. At any point in time, it is fairly simple to cost home ownership in the area where you are likely to want to live. Rental costs tend to follow house prices so whether you choose to own a home or not, you will need similar amounts of money to provide accommodation.

Accommodation and basic living expenses such as utilities (power, water, phone, etc.), groceries and transport (car or public) are the foundation of financial independence. Ask yourself whether you can provide these for yourself at present. If you are single, are you earning enough to cover your basic expenses? If you are in a relationship, could you do all this for yourself if your partner became disabled or if the relationship finished? Are you earning enough or able to earn enough to live life as you would want to on your own?

But you are likely to want to do more than eke out a basic existence. Consider some of the other things that are really important to you, such as time and money to visit family and friends, or funding for interests and entertainments. If you needed to, could you fund all of these projects by yourself?

*Colette is in her late forties. She and her partner live in a lovely clifftop home with fabulous views. He has his own business and they live a very comfortable lifestyle. Colette has a sales role that carries a $50,000 salary. When we looked at costing an independent life for Colette, she was quite surprised by the numbers.*

*Colette would want to continue to live in Melbourne. At a minimum, the kind of home she would want on her own would cost $800,000. When we added up the other 'basics' in her life, we estimated that she would need about $180,000 before tax to fund the kind of lifestyle that she would want as a minimum if she were on her own.*

*As Colette and Mike are still heavily mortgaged, she would only have about $150,000 if they separated and their home was sold.*

*Since we did this exercise, Colette has been working hard to ensure that her equity in the home and her earnings grow. The realisation that she would really struggle to live well independently has made her see that some things need to change.*

Women are sometimes nervous about taking some of the actions they need to get their financial plan underway. It can be hard at first to see yourself wearing all of the different 'hats' you need to make your business a success. At times you will have to be the CEO—for example, when you are thinking and planning for your future. At other times you will behave like the chief financial officer—setting budget targets, monitoring how your net worth is growing and taking corrective action when the numbers are not where you want them to be. When you are selecting members of your advisory team, you will behave more like the human resources director—you will want to interview people and check references.

Because women are socialised to behave in particular ways, it can be very difficult to see yourself taking on such diverse roles. One effective strategy is to 'call in the sisterhood'. It's like having an army of sisters or aunties or best friends who have all of the skills and attitudes needed to get the job done. We all do this: 'I'll ask Rose—she'll know how to get this to happen!'

I saw how well this strategy worked for my sister several years ago. She was managing a group of professionals—making appointments, chasing up clients, making sure that the professionals met their commitments, all the usual things that go on in a mid-size business. When I called her at work one day I was asked for my name and the receptionist seemed a little stressed when I gave it. I asked my sister why the response had been so strange. At that point she 'confessed' that whenever she had to chase up payments from clients, rather than deal with them under her usual name (Martha), she announced herself as 'Joan from Accounts'. There was no Accounts department, and of course no Joan! So unknown to me I had become the person who made the hard calls—while Martha had managed to maintain her wonderfully warm relationship with the clients.

It is often very difficult to play several roles, and you have to do it all the time in a smaller business. My sister had circumvented the problem by taking on a different persona and a different name. When she had to toughen up and ask people for money, she was no longer 'Mellow Martha' but 'Credit Controller Joan'!

Martha did not see herself as someone who would chase up the firm's debtors. She had a problem so she asked herself what was needed—and decided she needed Joan to do the tough stuff. (I am ten years older than her and had been working in business for a lot longer.) As I was on the other side of the world, she simply 'invented' me and got on the phone and asked for the bill to be paid just as she knew I would do.

This story is useful because it illustrates an important point: you may have to do many new and difficult things in order to take charge of your finances and become financially independent. It can be very hard to envisage yourself in some of those roles—such as dealing with an accountant, asking for a raise, investing in shares, negotiating a mortgage, saying 'no' to friends or family.

You have to believe that there is a part of you that is 'perfect' for whatever task you have to tackle to make sure that you achieve your goals. We are all accustomed to seeing ourselves and our friends in certain ways—for example, as organised, good with numbers, friendly, creative, anxious or practical. What if *you* could be all of these, if you could have any attributes you needed to be successful in your quest for financial independence?

All you would have to do then is decide which personality is in charge of which part of the project at any time. A handy way to do this is to give different aspects of your personality different names. You might, for example, put 'Creative Charlotte' in charge of coming up with a list of the things that are really important to you so that you know what you want to achieve. 'Administrative Anya' can be delegated the task of gathering the paperwork you need at your fingertips and devising a good filing system and work area. Each personality has its strengths and weaknesses—no one type does everything well. Your job is to choose the right personality for each task.

## SMART WOMAN STRATEGIES

A smart woman would plan the businesses of her life for the future:

- ♀ She would estimate the cost of the life she wants to lead, including accommodation, transport, basic expenses and some of the extras. She would work out the amount of money she would need to have or earn to sustain that lifestyle.
- ♀ She would then look at what she is worth right now, ascertaining the gap between her wealth and the cost of her planned lifestyle.
- ♀ She would look at how much she earns, how much she is able to earn and to what extent she can maintain the lifestyle she wants on her current earnings/wealth.
- ♀ She would decide which hats she needs to wear to make her businesses successful.
- ♀ She would work out which aspects of herself should wear which hat.
- ♀ She would give these 'sisters' some names for fun!

# 13 SETTING GOALS

Dreams and values are very powerful because that's where all your energy for change will come from. However, it's very difficult to take action on a dream or a value—by their very nature, they are rather vague and will mean different things to different people. In order to clarify what you want to happen and what you'll need to find the money for, you will need to set some specific goals.

Dreams—particularly clear ones—lead to goals. For example, if you have a dream of security, home ownership may well be an aspect of that dream. As you clarify that dream, you will have a picture of the type of house, the location, the value and the timing of the purchase that would meet your needs. You are then able to say clearly that you will buy a home of a certain market value with a certain deposit in a defined area within a defined time. It becomes very clear what you need to do. That is very motivating and really focuses you on what you need to do—you know exactly the target you are trying to hit.

All the evidence shows that women who set clear goals in writing have a far higher chance of achieving what they set out to do than those of us who have vague unwritten ideas of what we would like to be different. Over 20 years ago Harvard University did a study on the effect of written goals. They researched a group of graduating students and found that 84 per cent had no goals at all, 13 per cent had unwritten goals and 3 per cent had written down their goals. The researchers followed up the group ten years later: the 3 per cent who had written their goals were earning or were worth 10 times as much as the other 97 per cent.

The lesson is that setting goals and writing them down is very powerful in helping you achieve. Specific written goals will give you real focus. They will also provide a written plan that you can take action on today, tomorrow and the next day. Well-stated goals free you up to put all of your effort into executing the plan. You have done all of the thinking and planning down to the fine detail—now all you have to do is take action.

One of the best tips about goals is to make them SMART—that is, specific, measurable, attainable, relevant and time-bound. These terms provide a checklist to make sure that your goal is clear.

- ♀ *Specific* means detailed—if you want to own a house, you need to say what location, value, style, age, number of bedrooms, school zone, etc.
- ♀ *Measurable* refers to writing a goal in a way you can track—while you could not measure or track a goal of 'become more secure', you certainly can determine whether you buy a house that meets the above specifications.
- ♀ *Attainable* is a check on whether your goal has any realism—for example, if your house has a specified value of $2 million and your net worth at the moment is $50,000, that does not appear to be an attainable goal at any time in the foreseeable future. Not that you shouldn't dream big—you should. But you'd probably be better off considering a more modest house to start with.
- ♀ *Relevant* is a check on whether your goal is relevant to your dreams, values or other aspect of your project. Buying a house is relevant to the values of security and independence, but probably doesn't satisfy a value of spirituality or contribute to a project of lifelong personal development.
- ♀ *Time-bound* means that you have dates and deadlines. It's all too easy to let yourself off the hook by ignoring the timeline. If you have a goal to buy a house, good time-bound questions might include:

    - When will you have the deposit?

- When will you purchase?
- Over what period will you repay the mortgage?

The whole point of SMART goals is to pin yourself down so that all your questions are answered. Then you can get busy on the execution of your goal because you know the details. Following are some examples of SMART goals.

*Soraya's SMART goal for owning her home looks like this:*

- ♀ *Buy a three-bedroom detached house with verandah and garden in a suburb close to work. (Specific)*
- ♀ *Valued at between $300,000 and $350,000. (Measurable)*
- ♀ *Provide a $30,000 deposit (already have $20,000) and make monthly payments similar to my current rent. (Attainable)*
- ♀ *This will meet my value of security. (Relevant)*
- ♀ *Purchase home before the end of this year. (Time-bound)*

*Gretchen places a high value on her personal development and also on improving her prospects of employment and earning a higher income. Gaining a qualification is an appropriate goal in those circumstances. A SMART version looks something like this:*

- ♀ *Enrol in a correspondence course to complete a Diploma in Marketing. (Specific)*
- ♀ *Complete and pass the course with a C+ grade or better in each module. (Measurable)*
- ♀ *Accept offer of support from supervisor at work and apply for study leave time as per company policy. (Attainable)*
- ♀ *This will make me more employable, will probably get me a pay rise, and will allow me to be eligible for better positions with my current employer or others. (Relevant)*
- ♀ *Investigate options by the end of this month. Complete diploma within three years. (Time-bound)*

## SMART WOMAN STRATEGIES

A smart woman would set some clear goals for her future:

- ♀ She would start converting her values and dreams into specific goals.
- ♀ She would get a friend to help her clarify and make her goals as SMART as possible.
- ♀ She would write everything down so she can revisit these goals often to check how she is doing and update them.

# 14
# POWERING UP YOUR GOALS

You need to make sure your goals are as powerful as possible. People who succeed in any endeavour have very clear goals that they revisit constantly for inspiration and focus. Some of the other tips that smart women have found helpful when setting goals include the following six 'P's:

- ♀ Make your goals as *positive* as possible. We are often tempted to think about what we *don't* want, as in 'I don't want to end up as a lonely poor bag lady'. However, it is very difficult to take action on 'negative' goals. As much as possible, you want to turn them into positive statements—'I want to be an outrageously happy and fun-loving old lady with a Harley Davidson and the means to ignore any constraints my children might place on me!'
- ♀ State your goals in the *present* tense. This is because tomorrow never comes. Going back to an example in the last chapter, you might say: 'I have a diploma in marketing. I am in line for a pay rise and a promotion at work.' This helps you to start seeing yourself achieving your goal and your behaviour starts to move in the right direction. You see yourself feeling full of energy and confidence, standing up straight, reaching for the phone to take the next step . . . you get the picture!
- ♀ Make your goals *pressing* and *urgent*. This is related to stating them in the present tense. It is about setting deadlines, due dates and timelines. Some of the things will take years to achieve or are about your dreams for future decades. But, if at all possible, find some aspect that can be

addressed fairly quickly. A very useful aspect of this tip is to decide on something that can be done immediately or over the next 24 hours. This is particularly important with big goals like buying a house or getting a qualification—they can seem so big that they are overwhelming, and so we do nothing! If you can give yourself a pressing task to do immediately—for example: 'Go online and find at least three courses that would meet my needs before I go to bed'—you are far more likely to reach your goal because you will have the satisfaction and sense of achievement of making some progress *now*!

- ♀ Be as *precise* as you can. This is about pinning down enough detail so that there can be no 'fudging', 'waffle' or misunderstanding about what you intend to do.
- ♀ Make them *personal*. If you don't set the agenda very clearly for your life, others will do it for you. 'I' statements are very powerful—for example, 'I own my own home', 'I earn enough income to take care of me and the kids', ' I have a diploma in marketing', 'I play the flute', 'I am fit and full of energy'. Write down five 'I' statements of your own. Remember, these are not 'I shoulds' nor even 'I wishes': these are 'I am', 'I do' and 'I have' statements—and you'd better believe them!
- ♀ Have the goals *published*. There are several ways to approach this—and the more of them you use the better. As discussed already, you want to write them down. Putting them in writing makes them real and allows you to review them frequently (daily is preferable), and to revise and update them. Smart women might write them on a small wallet-sized card, and carry them in their bags, or laminate them and put them in the shower so they see them first thing in the morning. You can also publish by talking about them with friends and family. It may help your commitment if you share your goals—for instance, 'I am opening a savings account so that I can pay for music lessons.' Friends and family will then provide support for you in achieving your goal.

This may sound a little mechanistic—particularly if you have never written down goals before. But it really works. It's no accident that all good businesses commit their goals to paper and plan to invest (budget) to achieve those goals.

## SMART WOMAN STRATEGIES

A smart woman would use the six 'P's to add power to her goals:

- ♀ She would take each goal she has written and see whether she can make it even more powerful by using the six 'P's.
- ♀ She would enlist the help of a friend to challenge her on each of her goals to see how clear and how powerful they really are.

# PART IV

# TAKING CONTROL OF YOUR FINANCIAL FUTURE

# 15
# PLANNING FOR LIFETIME FINANCIAL INDEPENDENCE

Every woman needs her own individual plan to ensure that she can take care of herself financially for a lifetime. It's a great feeling to know that you are in control and that, even though life will inevitably have some difficult times, you will be able to take charge of your own decisions. Money does not solve everything by any means, but having your finances under control, and having some reserves, gives you many more options.

Remember, the whole point about being financially independent and smart with money is that you get the kind of life you want. Money will *never* be the most important thing in your life; rather, you need to be clear about what is of greatest importance to you and use your earning capacity and your money to make sure that your priorities get the energy and funding that they need.

In order to plan well, you need to have a clear view of your priorities. Some aspects of our lives are unavoidable, like paying for accommodation, transport and food. Others are more discretionary, like travel, hobbies or personal development. Things that one person considers essential for their happiness will be negotiable or of lesser importance to another. Personal finance plans need to be personal and individualised; however, the basic principles and framework are the same for all of us.

First there needs to be some *income*. Income usually comes from a job or some other form of work. However, you might be the beneficiary of a trust fund or you may own (or part-own) some rental properties or a business from which you get an income. What you do with this income will determine your ability to take care of yourself and make choices for yourself in the future. It's as simple as that.

So what should you do with the income? There are three main categories that your income must go into so that you can live today, look forward to tomorrow and know that your future will be secure.

1 *Investment*. This is in many ways both the most important and the most likely to be neglected. You are unlikely to be able to work for income right up until you die, so you must make provision for other income. Invested money today will provide income for future years. Investment can be under many headings—superannuation, property, mutual funds, direct share investments, deposits and so on. However, you can't leave investment until later as you need the time for your investments to grow. Your challenge in this category is to optimise your investments and to invest as much as you can as soon as you can. More about this later.
2 *Fixed expenses*. This is the stuff you have to pay for every day so that life can be lived. You'll be familiar with all the headings—accommodation, transport, food, clothing, medical care and so on. For many women this category is already taking everything—leaving no money for anything they want to do or for investment for the future. Your challenge in this category is to minimise your expenses. You really don't want to be spending a cent more on electricity, transport or telephone bills than you have to.
3 *Discretionary expenses*. This is the category where all the fun is. We're talking travel, entertainment, hobbies, leisure, sport here—and lots of things you don't *need* but *want*, like nice clothes, shoes, make-up, movies, eating out and many many more. This category is all too familiar for some because everything is being spent on these items—a particular trap for the young and single or busy working women. Your challenge here is to keep your head—what will you choose and plan for in this category while still allowing you to make some investments and cover your fixed expenses? You probably can't have it all so you need to choose carefully amongst the temptations in discretionary

spending. This is where it becomes really helpful to know what your dreams, values and priorities are.

Home ownership is a top priority for most women as a fixed expense. This will also represent your investment category in the early years. (Some women will have compulsory superannuation investment as well.) There are several good reasons for the choice of home ownership. We all have to live somewhere. It is very difficult to feel secure about the future if you are not confident that you will be able to afford accommodation—and housing and rental prices can get away from you quite easily. At some stage, you will need either to own your own home or be able to pay whatever is the going rate in rentals. Buying a house allows you to keep pace with the market—even if you don't live in it at the moment for whatever reason. It is also a form of compulsory saving. Your focus should be on repaying the mortgage as quickly as possible and then using surplus income to make other investments.

Why is this splitting of income so important? Well, it's too simplistic to say that all you need to do is budget for basics and save and invest the rest. After all, you not only want your money to last as long as you do; you also want to manage your income and spending so that you have and do the things that are most important to you as you live your life. Without a plan, we simply do the best we can each month and wonder why there is never enough left for any of the other things in life that we value. And investment will probably be overlooked altogether.

*Smart women know what's important to them, what they are willing to work hard for and where their spending priorities lie.*

Smart women are in the business of managing their lives; managing their money well is the means to ensuring that their lives are the best they can be. It is also much more exciting and interesting than simply approaching life as a budgeting exercise.

Revisit the various aspects of the 'pie' of life and what might be important to you in each area. What do you write that you want to achieve in the areas of work, family, social life, personal development, recreation, contribution, etc.? The clearer you are about what you want, the easier it will be to calculate your requirements for money. If you have a huge desire to travel extensively, for example, you will need to either forgo spending in other areas or resolve to increase your income to fund your travels. At the very least, you will be conscious of what takes priority and what the implications are for your income and expenditure.

Remember, you are planning to have the life you want, not just to make money.

## SMART WOMAN STRATEGIES

A smart woman would draw up plans for her life and her money:

- ♀ In line with her overall dreams, she would be as specific as possible about what she wants to be, do and have in her life.
- ♀ She would decide what takes priority. There will be non-negotiables like keeping body and soul together, but after that she has to make some real choices. She needs to think carefully about what she will choose and which trade-offs she is willing to make.

# 16 GROWING YOUR INCOME

Many women already have enough income from work or other sources to become financially independent. They may have a low net worth because they have never saved any of it to invest in assets that would grow their wealth and make them secure. Their challenge will be to change their spending habits and begin to invest rather than consume everything they earn.

However, other women may find themselves on very low incomes—if any at all. Even if you are very careful with spending and save everything you can, you may find the small sums needed to invest take a depressingly long time to accumulate.

It is all too simple when you are thinking and talking about money to focus only on the expenditure side—what you do with the money. However, you should also think about the income side—is there anything you can do to get more income?

Increasing your income will accelerate your path to financial fitness—the more income you have, the more you can save and invest, and the more secure you are for the rest of your life. And even an apparently small increase can make a very big difference.

Take a basic wage for unskilled work. Many women, at some stage in their lives, may earn $10 per hour. If you work a 40 hour week, that's $400 and if you work a full year you will earn $20,800. If you did that work for 40 years, you would earn $832,000 (ignoring tax for now).

If you could get a $1.50 an hour increase—which does not seem very much—the changes to the numbers are quite dramatic. You would now earn $460 a week ($60 extra). Your annual earnings would be $23,920 ($3,120 extra) and over a lifetime of 40 years you would earn $956,800. That's $124,800 extra.

It is worth looking at your own income and doing some calculations to see what difference an increase would make to your earnings. Try increases of 3, 5 and 10 per cent—and convince yourself that even relatively small increases are worth fighting for. Pay rates for a particular job rarely go backwards—they tend to get locked in. So look for every incresase you can get; that becomes the new baseline for the following year.

There are several strategies you can pursue to raise your income:

- ♀ *Get paid what I'm worth*. I noted earlier that, despite equal pay legislation, women typically earn less than men for the same work with the same qualifications. Do some research into what equivalent roles get paid in your organisation and elsewhere. If you are being paid less, talk to your manager about closing the gap. Ask your manager how pay levels are determined in your organisation. You'll be surprised at how often this works if you do your homework and have all the facts you need. You can check out equivalent jobs in other places by following up on ads in the paper or phoning a recruitment agency and asking about current rates for the work you do. Even a dollar or two extra an hour will make a big difference to what you can save—and you could be talking thousands of dollars a year, depending on your job. Women tend to get paid what they *settle for* rather than what they deserve to be paid—don't settle for less than you are worth.
- ♀ *Ask for a raise*. In my experience, women are far less likely to ask for a raise than men. Women often wait for management to take the initiative—and managers generally hate salary reviews so they often put them off. If you are a valued employee, your chances of a raise are very good—they won't want to lose you and they know it will cost them more than your pay rise to recruit a new person. Obviously you need to go about this in the right way and be ready to remind your manager of the contribution you are making and your achievements at work. They are not obliged to pay you more, but you are entitled to have your salary

reviewed regularly. Make sure it happens. Asking for a raise also sends a signal that you care and that you expect to be valued—that will be remembered the following year. And if you can do whatever it is that you are being paid for you can get yourself a raise! Don't be afraid to ask for more.

- ♀ *Get a new job*. It is often much easier to get a pay rise by changing jobs—either to a different organisation or to a different role. The biggest leaps in pay are usually achieved by changing your job—a new employer usually feels obliged to offer more. By the time they reach the point of making you a job offer, they have already invested a lot of time and money in the process. They have seen the other available candidates and they want *you*. This is the best time to look for an increase in pay—unless your request is outrageous for the role, and for your skill and experience level, you'll probably be successful. In my experience, women often feel that they can only accept or decline the job offer; men negotiate for what they want. And mostly they get a lot more than was initially offered. So polish up your CV, have a good audit of your skills and experience and go looking for a better job with better pay. Keep an eye on the situations vacant pages in the paper or on websites and get a clear sense of what employers are looking for that you are able to offer. Often the longer you stay in a job the less notice anyone takes—it can be much easier to make an impression and be properly valued by a new employer.
- ♀ *Make myself more valuable*. In the end, employers pay for the knowledge, skills and the track record you bring to their business. No matter how you earn money—even if you don't rate it very highly—you should treat your work as a career. It pays to take every opportunity you can to learn more. Ask your manager for training and take every opportunity to learn new skills—both on the job at work and on any courses that are on offer. Volunteer for new tasks and projects. Get a reputation for being flexible, willing and quick to take on new tasks. These attributes can be as highly valued in the workplaces as hard skills.

- ♀ *Invest in myself.* Some organisations and industries are much better at developing their employees than others. While a good employer will invest in your training, your future is your responsibility. It makes great financial sense for you to invest in yourself. This might mean paying for some additional study, going on a course or buying yourself a PC so that you can improve your skills. If it applies to your area of work, take the time to read books and listen to tapes that will help you be better at what you do. Investing time and money in your own development will give you a very good payoff over time. It is never too late—and it's never too early either—to start to make yourself more employable and more valuable. And you should never stop—this isn't just a good idea for young people. Choose to learn in order to earn.

Even on relatively low wages and salaries, the average person earns hundreds of thousands of dollars over a lifetime. If you can get your hourly or annual pay increased even by a small amount, you will not only benefit this year, but could be multiplying it by 40 hours a week and 52 weeks a year for the rest of your working life. When you use that money for savings and investment, it will make a huge difference to your future. Do the sums and see what a difference even a small increase would make to your current earnings.

The majority of women are stuck in work that pays poorly or at best an average income. I am constantly amazed at how little difference in effort stands between work that pays $10 an hour and work that pays $100 an hour. It is often only a qualification that a woman is perfectly capable of getting. Sometimes it's just acquired skills and experience along the way. At other times, it's just reward for taking the risk to work for yourself. If you have the skills to manage small children well, for example, there probably isn't a sales, customer service or people management job that you couldn't excel at.

Some women, for whatever reason, may not be able to increase income through a job outside the home. It is still worth considering what you can do to earn money. The market for work from home has increased enormously in recent years. Do you have skills or time you could be paid for? Many women who are at home with small children choose to mind another child for pay. Childcare is expensive, and many facilities offer very limited hours of care so there is quite a demand for private care. Alternatively, you may have word processing skills and can do accounts or other office work from home. Believe in yourself—if you have the skills to run a home or if you have ever been in paid work you almost certainly have some skills you can use at home that others will pay for.

A period at home can provide an opportunity to grow your skills so that you are more valuable when you return to the workforce. Some women also use the opportunity to plan and get started in a business of their own. While this can take some time to be profitable, the payoff is that you get to keep all the profits—you're the owner as well as the worker.

Many of the smart women I know raised their first investment stake by finding something they could sell to get some income. Some rented out a room or garage that they weren't using. Others held garage sales and sold *everything* they no longer used—old sports equipment, children's toys, unused furniture, kitchen appliances they bought and didn't use—and many of their other spending mistakes! One smart woman solved her untidy teenager's problem by announcing she would sell any of his stuff he left lying around—a double whammy! She was serious. There's nothing like the feeling of getting that first lump sum together so that you can invest.

No matter how you choose to earn money, it's good to think of growing income as if you were a business. You are in the business of managing a great life and managing your money so that you can have a good life. So treat the whole idea of growing income as if you were funding this business seriously. It's a decision for life. Once you start looking for ways to increase income, you will be surprised at how many you can come up with—whatever your circumstances today.

## SMART WOMAN STRATEGIES

A smart woman would get creative about increasing her income by:

- ♀ getting a job;
- ♀ getting a better job;
- ♀ asking for a raise;
- ♀ making herself worth more to her employer;
- ♀ selecting a way to earn income while at home;
- ♀ seeing if she can sell something;
- ♀ asking herself: 'What can I do to raise my income?'
- ♀ asking herself: 'How can I make myself more valuable?'

# 17
# WHAT SMART WOMEN DO WITH THEIR INCOME

No matter how much or how little income you have now, what you decide to do with it is critical to your financial independence for the rest of your life. If you read no other chapter in this book, this one can change your life for the better forever.

Most of us take our money and and spend it, intending to save whatever is left. But with this strategy, there's usually nothing left so we don't save, we have no investments and our net worth is likely to be low—restricting our level of choice and independence. Even women who earn very well often spend everything that they earn—and more. Many of the women I've coached have admitted that they have been paid very well for years—but have never realised that they must *save* some of it!

> What you do with your after-tax income will determine the quality of your life and your ability to be independent.

If there is one secret to a better financial future, it is that you must spend *less* than your income. Smart women handle their income differently by using the following strategies.

- ♀ *Smart women create a surplus*. No matter how little your income is, you must not consume it all. This can be extremely difficult initially—either because you earn so little or because you have a habit of spending everything you earn. It is the money that you *don't* consume that will improve your future. This principle cannot be overstated: your financial independence tomorrow depends on avoiding spending all of your income today. So, no matter what your level of income is, your fixed expenses (rent, food, etc.) plus your discretionary expenses (entertainment, hobbies, etc.) need to add up to less than 100 per cent of your income. If you have money left over, you have created a surplus. If your income is very low, this surplus may only be 5–10 per cent of your total after-tax income; if you are a high earner (or have other sources of income), then that surplus could be 20, 30 or even 50 per cent. In other words, some women who are low earners will consume 90–95 per cent of their income, while others will only need to spend 50–80 per cent of their income. Clearly, if you have a high income, your opportunity to create a larger surplus is easier. But you *must* create a surplus. You *cannot* become financially independent if you consume all of your income.

♀ *Smart women pay themselves first.* Instead of spending first and planning to save a surplus, smart women turn this pattern on its head. They take a preplanned amount, no matter how small, and they put it aside as savings so that they can invest it to fund their independence and life choices for the future. No matter how small this amount might be to begin with—even $10 per week—the principle is important and the habit it develops becomes lifelong and precious. And no one else will do this for you. You change everything once you start to pay yourself first.

♀ *Smart women pay off debts.* Smart women use the surplus they create to pay off debt as a priority. They pay off the debt that carries the highest interest rate first—this debt is costing them the most per $100 borrowed. If you have run up credit card debt (or other consumption borrowings), you need to devote as much as possible of your income to getting rid of this debt first. That's because it tends to carry very high interest rates (up to 20 per cent), so every month it is not repaid it costs you more and more. It is also 'bad' debt in the sense that you have borrowed for items or services that you have consumed (such as meals, clothes, entertainment, etc.); these are things that won't make you better off or financially independent.

This debt is very different than borrowing for something like a house, which not only maintains its value but will probably become more valuable—thus raising your net worth and making you more independent in the future.

If you have a mortgage, it is a good idea to use the surplus income you have created to pay off your mortgage as quickly as possible. If you can create any more income—a second job, a pay rise, a tax refund, an inheritance—then the very best thing you can do with it is to use it to pay off your mortgage (debt) as quickly as possible.

♀ *Smart women allocate money for living*. Once you have created a surplus and used it to pay debt—or, if debt-free, invested it—money needs to be allocated for the fixed expenses of life—rent, electricity, phone, food, transport, clothing, and so on. Much of this is unavoidable but smart women seek to minimise expenditure here. When you do your audit, you may be horrified at some of your bills in this area and will resolve to trim phone bills, grocery expenses, etc. This is simply about freeing up money for things that are more important to you.

♀ *Smart women then allocate money for goals*. You have paid yourself first (money for saving and investing for the future) and covered the essentials of living. Now some funds can be devoted to some of those activities that you determined you would like to do, be or have. These probably can't all be done immediately—you will need to work out priorities and timing. And each of your goals will need its own plan (budget), or it too will run out of control. You may, for example, have decided that an overseas trip is very important to you. To achieve this goal, you may have worked out that you need to wait for three years and save an extra $5000 over and above the money you are investing for the future. You might also have chosen to take up hill walking as a hobby to meet both wellness and social values—and thus need to allocate $300 for boots and $200 for trips in the coming year.

♀ Smart women take charge of their financial future. This is *your* money, so you need to allocate it in priority order to the things that will make your life better today and tomorrow and to allow you to be independent for the rest of your life.

♀ *Smart women are businesslike.* I have seen women go from being totally useless with money to behaving like financial controllers. They have their plan, they track what is spent and they look at how they are doing each week or each month, depending on how often they receive income. They basically hold themselves accountable for making the plan happen—it's almost as if they are reporting to themselves each month.

You may well be reading this and thinking that this is great advice for a woman who earns a lot of money but that you are not in that category and that this has no relevance to you. Not so. The principles here work no matter how much or how little income you have to begin with. These are great principles for financial independence—even if you only have pocket money to work with.

> Smart women spend money they earn, on stuff they really care about, to meet their own expectations and plans for a financially independent life.

Let's put it another way: *it's the surplus that counts.* And your job is to create a 'surplus' before you spend anything. Your financial independence rests on your commitment to putting money aside—even if it is just a little at first—to save and invest.

To achieve a surplus, you may need to rethink the way you spend money. Smart women learn how to spend well! Start to plan for larger expenditures like appliances, and take care to buy better quality. This simply means becoming more *mindful* about what you do with your money. Society is conspiring to make us '*mindless*' in how we use our income. Marketers spend vast sums convincing us that we must have their products and services in order to have a 'good' life. It is so easy to spend money we really don't have on stuff we don't care about very much to meet expectations we don't really agree with anyway. The secret of 'mindful' spending is to be very clear about what is truly important to us and to spend in line with our priorities.

Taking back control of your money is largely about making sure your spending is in line with your plans for financial independence. Make sure that you get more of what you *really* want with your income—financial independence for life, a secure future, and a worry-free present that includes some of the having, being and doing that is important to you.

## SMART WOMAN STRATEGIES

A smart woman would decide what she was going to do with her income:

- ♀ She would allocate her income in line with her priorities, ensuring that she puts some aside before she spends any.
- ♀ She would decide in advance how much can be spent in which categories.
- ♀ She would work on becoming a 'smart' spender, moving from mindless to mindful spending.

# 18
# ALLOCATING YOUR INCOME

Once you've made the commitment to create a surplus, you will need to allocate actual dollar amounts to the categories of investment, fixed and discretionary expenses.

Experts often suggest that people should save 10 per cent of their income and live on the rest. However, that may not work for everyone. Fixed expenses are often very difficult to cover on a lower income and, at least initially, women on a lower income may be able to invest only a small percentage of their income. However, if you want to achieve financial independence you do have to work to get that percentage up, whether by managing your fixed and discretionary expenses more tightly or by growing your income.

Smart women often find it helpful to think in percentages in order to see the big picture when it comes to dividing their income. On lower earnings, fixed expenses will take a higher proportion of income, leaving less for discretionary spending. This will be true both in percentage and dollar terms.

*Laila has an after-tax income of $35,000. She is a sole parent with a two-year-old child. Needless to say, her fixed expenses threaten to take every cent. However, she is absolutely committed to becoming financially independent. She has decided after a lot of dreaming and goal-setting that her income will be split as follows:*

Laila's income allocation

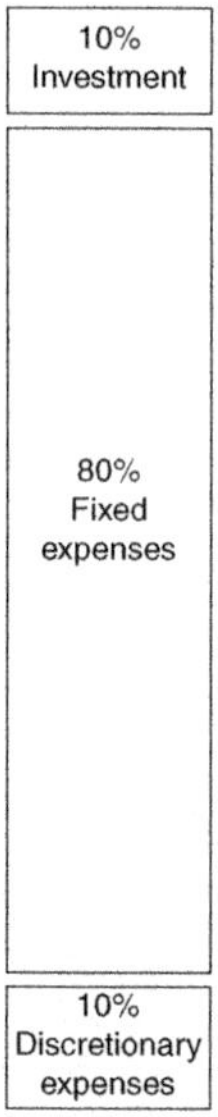


*In practice, this means that Laila will save $3,500 per year ($290 per month, or $67 per week). She will allow herself and her son to spend the same amount ($67 a week) on discretionary expenses. This will have to cover all outings, recreation and treats. All of her fixed expenses, such as rent, food, transport, electricity, and so on will have to come out of the remaining $28,000, which comes to $538 a week. While this will never be easy, Laila is certain that the reward of financial independence and a better life in the future will be worth it. She is saving through an automatic payment from each pay period.*

Perhaps the biggest hurdle when you begin your path to financial independence is creating the surplus that will change your financial position forever. That can look almost impossible—you may already seem to be spending everything you earn—or worse, even more than you earn, so that you are building debt. However, there is no easy way around this obstacle—somehow, fixed and discretionary spending have to be reduced to create a surplus that can be saved. At this point, a smart woman takes out her calculator and goes through all of the information she has on how she currently spends her income. She will look for every dollar that does not have to be consumed in fixed expenses. She will get tough on discretionary expenses and really limit that consumption. The payoff, of course, is knowing that she now has an account somewhere accumulating money that is tagged for her future happiness, her security and her dreams. The percentages vary as income rises or circumstances change.

*Jenna earns $50,000 per annum after tax. She is single and has no children. She has always held down a good job and works hard. Jenna has been living a very social and fun lifestyle—she has an up-market rented apartment and she enjoys frequent holidays and weekends away. Jenna knows that this is no recipe for independence in the future and, at 38, has decided that she must start to build her investments so that her future decades will be good. She has decided to split her income in the following proportions:*

Jenna's income allocation

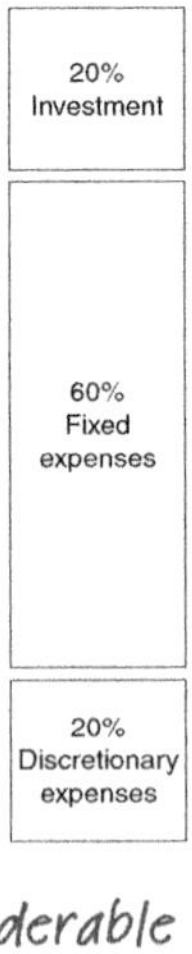


*Jenna can, with some considerable lifestyle sacrifices (such as more modest accommodation and fewer trips), save 20 per cent of her income. This will amount to $10,000. She will pare back her fixed expenses so that she can consume 20 per cent on discre-*

*tionary items that she will choose in line with her stated dreams. She will still be able to spend $192 a week on discretionary activities. She will need to save a big proportion of this for several months before she can afford the overseas holiday she wants. Jenna is quite excited about the prospect of having $10,000 at the end of her first year of saving, even though she knows it will mean big changes in how she lives. All of the impulsive purchases will have to go and the social whirl will have to be reduced. However, Jenna can see that she will have a deposit for a house quite quickly if she sticks to her plan.*

Some women have very high incomes by any standards—but still very little net worth. It is all too easy to allow consumption to rise with income. We can all remember surviving on a shoestring at some time, but as income rises we all seem to spend more. So the equation remains the same—100% income = 100% spending. No matter how much you earn, this pattern takes you nowhere. It can feel good for a while—you have a great life, buy lots of stuff, go out a lot, and seem well off. At the back of most women's minds, however, there will be a niggle—you may look and behave as if you are 'rich', but you know you are not. There is no net worth building—all of the income is going to sustain your lifestyle.

Many professional women fall into this pattern. Their incomes rise rapidly with experience and promotions. They also find it easy to convince themselves that high consumption is 'expected' of them—smart accommodation, badged car, designer clothes, exotic holidays, plenty of expensive socialising. Believe me, you can spend *any* amount of income easily! Some of the women I have worked with can get through hundreds of thousands of dollars each and every year like this—and with nothing to show for it in assets.

Obviously, if you are lucky enough to have a high income, you can make dramatic changes to your financial position very quickly. Even if you have been consuming every last cent you have the level of income that will allow you to accumulate savings very fast if you choose to change your approach and habits.

Sarah is an accountant. She has an after-tax income of $120,000. Even though she understands the numbers, and manages her clients' affairs very well, she has totally neglected her own finances. Sarah is 35 and single. She always expected to be married by now with some cute kids, a nice home and a golden retriever. However, despite some long-term relationships, she is now alone. Finally, Sarah is confronting the fact that she may well be solely responsible for her financial future. This has come as something of a shock. Sarah feels a bit of a fool—after all, she is a professional accountant and can hardly claim that she does not understand money and numbers. However, Sarah has decided to change the situation fast! She intends to divide her income as follows:

Sarah's income allocation

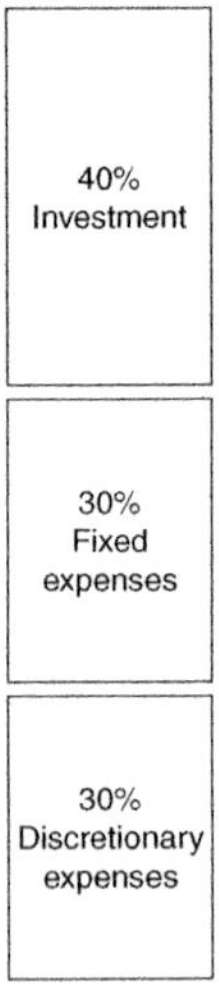


This will mean that Sarah can save $48,000 each year. She already owns her home but has more than $200,000 to pay on the mortgage. Initially, Sarah will devote every dollar of savings to paying off her mortgage as quickly as possible. Then she intends to invest in shares and grow her net worth as aggressively as she can. She may still get the cute kids, a nice home *and a golden retriever or she may not, but financially it won't matter.*

The examples above show that there is no set percentage that should be adopted for saving. Ten per cent is minimal, particularly if your income is low. On a lower income, even 10 per cent will not be a great amount in a dollar sense and it will take a long time to accumulate much money. However, if you are lucky enough to earn well, you should be saving a higher percentage—perhaps 20–50 per cent of income depending on your particular circumstances.

The key to your financial independence is to create a surplus of income that can be saved or invested. Ten per cent can seem impossible to some women at first. But ask yourself whether you really, really want life to change. If you work 40 hours a week, 10 per cent represents only half a day's earnings. If you work an eight-hour day, it's less than an hour's earnings each day. Isn't your financial independence and future important enough for this? The real difficulty tends not to be the dollars involved, but that we become so accustomed to consuming everything we earn, no matter how large or small our income may be. This is the mindset that has to change before you can become financially independent.

Look at it another way: choose something you habitually spend on—chocolate bars, coffee, magazines, etc. If you gave up that habit, how much could you save each week or month? If you are a cigarette smoker, buy lunch every day or open a new bottle of wine every night, you will have a lot of potential 'surplus' to draw on without affecting any essentials.

Some women find it fun to pick one of these beloved expenditures and, rather than feel they are 'giving up', add up what they spend in that area and reallocate it to something specific—like shares, a house deposit or a holiday. It's a lot easier to forgo some of the things that are consuming your dollars if you are firmly focused on something you really want instead.

Not spending on something today becomes easier and more meaningful when you have a clear goal in mind. It is easy then to imagine yourself saying:

'I can't do lunch. I have to go to Noumea (next year!).'
'Sorry, I don't want to see the movie. I am doing a diploma in design on Fridays.'
'I won't be going window shopping on Saturday morning—we're "shopping" for a house instead.'

As time goes on, continue to analyse how you are dividing your income. If you receive a promotion or increase in salary, it is important that you don't allow your consumption to rise in line with the income. Consumption rises with income—the more we have the more we want. Take your increase in income and immediately add it to your savings component, keeping your fixed and discretionary expenses as they are. This will be relatively painless as long as you never let yourself get used to having—and spending—the extra income.

Similarly, if you get a one-off windfall, such as a bonus or a legacy, devote it to savings. If you have a mortgage, use the lump sum to pay off some of the mortgage. You will reduce your debt and shorten the term of the loan, which will save on interest payments. Lumps of additional money, well invested, can make a very big difference to your net worth.

## SMART WOMAN STRATEGIES

A smart woman would decide how she was going to divide her income:

- ♀ She would first decide what percentage of her income to save.
- ♀ Then she would split the remaining income between fixed and discretionary expenses.
- ♀ Finally, she would commit any additional income—such as pay rises or bonuses—to her savings category, keeping fixed and discretionary expenses at the same level as before.

# 19
# INDEPENDENCE THROUGH INVESTING

Never feel that you have too little income or are not smart enough to be an investor. There are not too many 'must do' activities in finance, but investing is one of them. (The others are that you must have some income, and you must keep some of it as surplus.)

Saving is vital if you intend to have any freedom or choices in the future. If you have to depend on the state to support you, it won't feel like choice, freedom or independence—if you want any of these, you will have to provide them for yourself. This is unlikely to change in the future—indeed, all the evidence points to the situation becoming even worse.

It is important to keep some savings in the bank so that you can deal with difficult times or emergencies such as a sudden death in your family, illness or unemployment. At times like this people can't work—often for weeks. Your income might stop, depending on what you do, but your expenses keep going up. You might have to make plane trips or deal with frightening medical bills.

Bad things do happen and you have to have some money set aside that you can get your hands on relatively easily—otherwise the bad times will be even worse. The last thing you want to do is put these expenses on your credit card. Estimates vary but the experts tend to agree that you need about three months' living costs saved and easily accessible. But while you do need some readily accessible savings in cash for emergencies, that's not where most of your savings should be.

The whole point of investing is that you take some of the money you have allocated for this purpose and use it to make

> Make your money work as hard for you as you had to work to earn it.

more. In other words, you don't let it sit in the bank on a low interest rate hoping that it will be worth enough when you come to use it. Instead, you need to look for a higher return than the bank will ever pay you in interest. Even 1 or 2 per cent more each year will make a very large difference over the years.

In addition, your investment will *compound*. This means that, as your investment makes money, that extra money is also invested. So the interest, or money, you have earned is earning its own interest as well. This has a really profound effect on the total amount of your investment after a number of years.

Let's have a closer look at how this works, because it is one of the most important things about money that you can ever learn.

Let's say you have $1,000 to 'invest' and can get a rate of 10 per cent per annum. If you invest your $1,000, you will get $100 of interest. You can spend the interest ($100) and invest the $1,000 the following year and get another $100, which you can take, spend, whatever. This is called *simple* interest: you continue to have the same amount of capital ($1,000); you continue to invest it at whatever rate you can get (10 per cent here); and you earn a sum of interest ($100 here) which you take and use however you wish. At the end of ten years, you have your capital—$1,000—and you have also earned ten lots of $100—another $1,000. You have $2,000 in total.

It looks like this:

| Year | Capital | Interest rate | Interest earned | Interest spent | Total at year end |
|---|---|---|---|---|---|
| 1 | $1000 | 10% | $100 | $100 | $1000 |
| 2 | $1000 | 10% | $100 | $100 | $1000 |
| 3 | $1000 | 10% | $100 | $100 | $1000 |
| 4 | $1000 | 10% | $100 | $100 | $1000 |

| | | | | | |
|---|---|---|---|---|---|
| 5 | $1000 | 10% | $100 | $100 | $1000 |
| 6 | $1000 | 10% | $100 | $100 | $1000 |
| 7 | $1000 | 10% | $100 | $100 | $1000 |
| 8 | $1000 | 10% | $100 | $100 | $1000 |
| 9 | $1000 | 10% | $100 | $100 | $1000 |
| 10 | $1000 | 10% | $100 | $100 | $1000 |

Now look at the difference if you *compound* the interest—that is, add the interest earned each year back into the capital sum and reinvest the new amount.

| Year | Capital | Interest rate | Interest earned | Interest spent | Total at year end |
|---|---|---|---|---|---|
| 1 | $1000.00 | 10% | $100 | $100 | $1100.00 |
| 2 | $1100.00 | 10% | $110 | $110 | $1210.00 |
| 3 | $1210.00 | 10% | $121.00 | $121.00 | $1331.00 |
| 4 | $1331.00 | 10% | $133.10 | $133.10 | $1464.10 |
| 5 | $1464.10 | 10% | $146.40 | $146.40 | $1610.50 |
| 6 | $1610.50 | 10% | $161.00 | $161.00 | $1771.50 |
| 7 | $1771.50 | 10% | $177.20 | $177.20 | $1948.70 |
| 8 | $1948.70 | 10% | $194.80 | $194.80 | $2143.50 |
| 9 | $2143.50 | 10% | $214.40 | $214.40 | $2357.90 |
| 10 | $2357.90 | 10% | $235.80 | $235.80 | $2593.70 |

What is the difference between simple and compound interest? Why does one investor have $2,593.70 while the other only has the original $1,000? The answer is that one has taken out the interest each year and spent it. The other has left the interest in the system and let it compound so that there is interest earned on the interest. If you think this is an insignificant amount, try the example with an investment of several thousand dollars.

Investment is the real key to financial independence. Unless you are on a huge salary or inherit money, you are unlikely to have any financial independence unless you invest. You can live within your income this year and feel quite satisfied, but what are you going to do when you stop working? You may be living well now because your partner has a very high income, but what are you going to do if he or she dies or leaves or becomes unemployed?

Investment is all about setting money aside today to create more money for tomorrow. And remember that it's not the money itself that matters, but what the money will allow you to do. Financial independence is all about having choices.

> You don't have to be rich to invest, but if you don't invest you won't be rich!

Saving and investing is mostly just a habit—once you will soon learn to love! Many of the women I coach astonish themselves about how quickly they become passionately interested in investment once they start enjoying the satisfaction of all the life choices and independence their investment promises for the future.

No matter how little you have, it is never too early to begin. And it is never too late either. No matter how little you can set aside, investing it well will mean there is more tomorrow and therefore your level of choice and independence will be greater. Give up that daily cappuccino, say 'no' to the glass of wine after work, cut down café lunches to one a week or give up your expensive flower habit and put that money to work for your future. Even if your money is only saved in bank deposits, you will be amazed at how much it will grow. Invest it for a better return for several years and you will be astounded.

## SMART WOMAN STRATEGIES

A smart woman would decide that from now on she is an investor:

- ♀ She would find some money, no matter how little, that can be set aside on a regular basis for investing.
- ♀ She would keep looking at compound interest tables until she is convinced what a good idea it is to save a little regularly and invest it, then reinvest the interest too.

# 20
# THE BASICS OF INVESTMENT

This is not meant to be a book about *how* and *where* to invest your money. However, many women don't know where to begin. Finance seems to be full of technical terms and impenetrable jargon—but that's all it is, jargon. The ideas underneath are surprisingly straightforward.

We pay a very big price for being afraid of jargon. When we are afraid we do nothing, but the basics of investment are very simple and basic investment strategies are all we need to be very successful.

When you strip all the jargon away, investing is simply about taking some money and using it to create more. There are only three things that really matter:

1 the amount you invest;
2 the interest rate on the investment; and
3 the length of time you invest it for.

Each of these variables is very important, however.

It's a good idea to have a play with some of the sums so that you start to feel more comfortable with what happens to money when you invest it. Let's take an example from the last chapter. You have $1,000 to invest. Imagine that you can get a 10 per cent return (i.e. your investment will pay you 10 per cent interest per annum). That means that, at the end of the year, your money will have earned $10 for every $100 you invested. If you leave the interest there, next year you will earn 10 per cent on $1,100, and it will continue to compound.

These may seem like small increases, but over time reinvesting the interest means that your investment grows a great deal. In jargon, this is known as 'compounding'. The crucial part is leaving your investment alone to compound for as long as you can. Then it really takes off.

Compounding

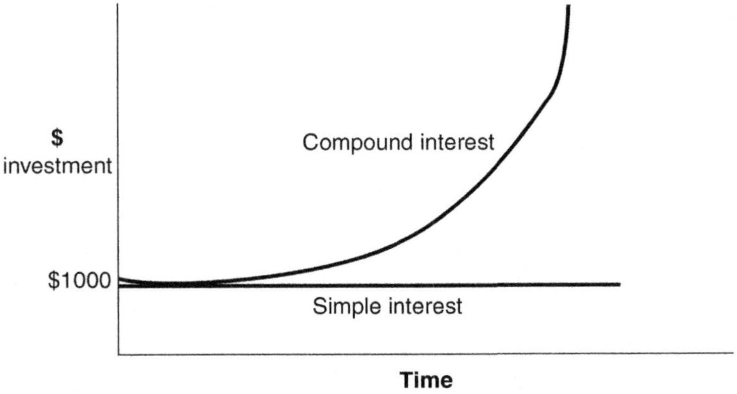


Understanding compounding is probably the most important thing that any woman needs to know about investing money.

All three variables (the amount you invest, the rate you invest at and the length of time you invest it for) make a big difference to the results:

♀ The *amount* you invest makes a very real difference. However, even if you are only at the beginning of your path to wealth and have very little to invest, do begin. Compounding works so well that there is no reason to delay.

- ♀ The *rate of interest* also makes a huge difference. Try the above examples using interest rates of 9, 10 and 12 per cent and note the impact of even 1 per cent difference.
- ♀ And *time* is your most important ally. It is only as time goes on that you will really see the huge gains of compounding—the early years don't look that spectacular but ultimately the effect is huge. Compounding begins slowly but snowballs. Most people don't wait long enough to get the real benefits.

You might like to play with these figures on a simple calculator. Key in ($1,000 × 1.10 =) to add on 10 per cent. Then, with your answer ($1,100), do the same again ($1,100 × 1.10 =) and you will get $1,210. You can keep going to see how quickly this builds up.

If you find all of this exciting, you should get a financial calculator which will allow you to do these types of calculations quickly without going through so many steps.

## SMART WOMAN STRATEGIES

A smart woman would decide that from now on she is an investor:

- ♀ She would decide how much she can invest on a regular basis.
- ♀ She would invest regularly.
- ♀ She would reinvest any money she made.

# 21
# THE THREE INVESTMENTS

There are only three places where you can invest your money successfully:

> *1 property;*
> *2 business (shares); and*
> *3 interest-bearing deposits.*

The definition of an investment is that it carries a return. So avoid 'investing' in art, antiques, jewellery, or at the racecourse. None of these is an investment. Investments carry a return—they generate income. You might or might not get a change in the value of the asset itself, but that is not income. So-called investment in art and antiques or classic cars is speculation—you are hoping that the asset will go up in value. It might; it might not. But you can be certain that there will be no income.

When you cut through all of the hype and jargon of the financial world, the only three things that will give you a cash return are property, business and interest-bearing deposits. You make your money in property and business (shares) by owning the asset and taking the profits. You make money in interest-bearing deposits by lending your money and being paid for that (interest). Owning property and business is riskier and therefore usually gives a higher return. Lending your money is less risky, and therefore you usually get a lower return.

All of the other investments that you hear about—like unit trusts, shares, superannuation funds, managed funds and group investment funds are simply *means* of investing in property, business or interest-bearing deposits.

You can either invest *directly* in property, business or interest-bearing deposits, or you can pool your money with others and invest in various funds that are managed by professionals—you do not have to choose the properties, businesses or deposits yourself.

Many women choose to invest directly in property by purchasing houses or flats. One of the reasons that women like this form of investment is that it is reasonably easy to borrow to buy residential property. Another reason is that managing residential property often fits in with the rest of a woman's life. We feel that we understand residential property—after all, we live in homes; we have bought and sold them; we know what other women want in a property. Most women who want to invest in industrial (warehouses), commercial (offices) or retail (shops) property will need to wait until they have high net worth or else invest in these forms of property through property investment funds.

Other women will be attracted to investing in business (shares). The sharemarket can seem very bewildering. But shares are simply a means of investing in business. You probably can't raise enough capital to buy Microsoft—but you can own a share of them (and a share of their profits). Again, you can do this directly by choosing businesses that you would like to invest in and purchasing shares through a sharebroker or online. Obviously, you will want to learn about the business you are interested in and how the sharemarket works (more knowledge and skills), but this is a very worthwhile effort. You can still invest in business (shares) without any of this work by investing in managed funds that in turn invest in shares. You can even choose particular funds that concentrate in certain types of business—for example, pharmaceutical, natural resources, infrastructure. You will own units in the fund; the fund will own shares in the businesses. Professional fund managers do all the work.

Interest-bearing deposits are the third option. Many women think of these as simply putting their money in the bank. But, just like property and business, there is far more behind the term—bank deposits, bonds, mortgage income trusts, and so on.

Obviously, you could spend the rest of your life studying investment and all of the options available. And many people do—that's their interest or their job. However, you don't need to do this unless you want to. If you wish to own property or shares directly, you will want to inform yourself about the property markets and the sharemarkets. And you would be well advised to buy some books, go to some courses and even join some associations like a share club or a property investors' group. But you can still be an investor without doing any of this. You can invest in various funds that will do all of the choosing and managing for you.

The reason that you need to invest some of your money in things other than bank deposits is that you will earn a bigger return—in other words, more interest or profit. Over longer periods, property and shares give better returns than putting your money in the bank. But property and shares are riskier—the property market and the sharemarket grow well over the longer term but from year to year they can be up or down, and sometimes swing quite dramatically. This is called volatility and it looks like this:

Investment Returns (Short-term)

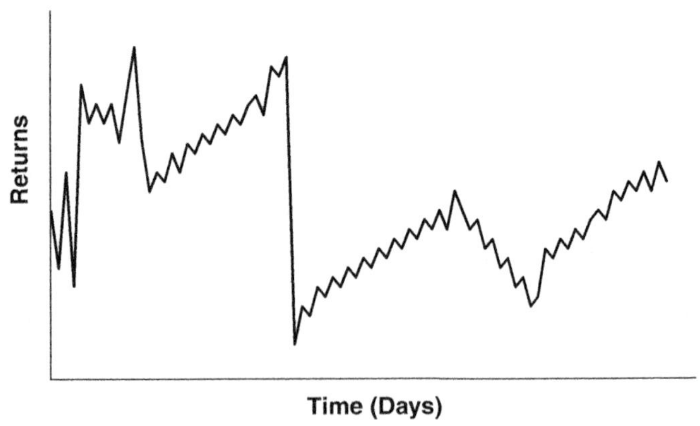


This is what the markets can look like from day to day or week to week. You don't notice it as much with property as shares because property is not traded every day the way shares are. It is easy to get very unnerved about volatility. However, if you look at what property and share markets do over a longer period, the graph looks a lot smoother—and less frightening:

Investment Returns (Long-term)

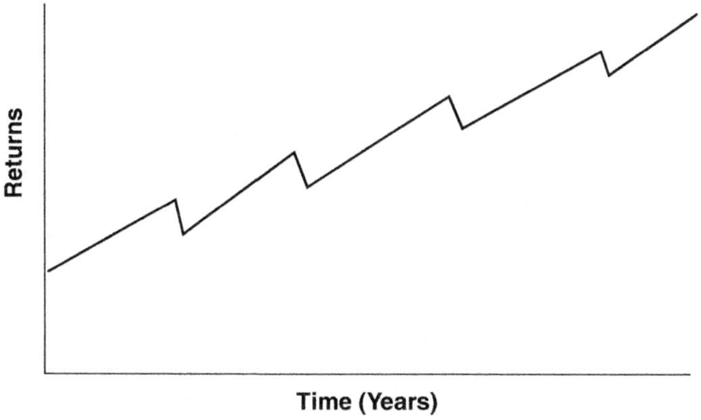


On the one hand, you do need to have some of your money invested in higher return assets than bank deposits. Your bank deposits will not earn enough interest to grow your money (compound) quickly enough. So your net worth (money lifeline) will not grow high enough to give you financial independence.

On the other hand, you probably can't afford to have all of your money invested in volatile markets. It is unwise to put money into the property market or sharemarket that you will need access to in less than five years. If you have to withdraw it, your timing may coincide with a low period in the market and you will lose a lot of your money. You will have seen many people over the last year or two take their money back from the sharemarket and suffer big losses. You may also have seen someone forced to sell a house at a bad time in the market. It also costs to enter and exit these markets—so you need to stay long enough to make these transaction costs worthwhile. Just consider the costs involved in buying and selling a house. You can't afford to keep changing your mind.

So what should you invest in? Smart women diversify their investments. That means that they spread their investment money across the three classes of investment—some in deposits, some in property and some in business (shares). This spreads the risk that you might choose the wrong investment for that period. In other words, smart women don't put all of their eggs in one basket. The easiest way to do this, unless you want to take an active interest in investment, is to invest through funds. This is a great way to begin and you can get more directly and actively involved as your knowledge and skill grow.

And that's about all you need to know about investment to achieve financial independence. All the rest is only jargon.

You don't need to be an expert in finance to be a successful investor—all you need is some regular money and some time to wait for it to grow. And you do not need to have a lot of money to be an investor. It works the other way round: you get to have a lot of money *because you invest.*

Experts that I talk to say that women make very successful investors once they start. Research indicates that women who invest read about prospective investments and seek good advice. They do their homework. Once they commit to regular savings and investments they keep their commitments. And, most importantly, they don't keep changing their minds! Men, it seems, typically throw money into investments when the market is at a high and withdraw them when it is low—exactly the opposite of what you need to do. As someone once said, dollars do better when they are accompanied by sense!

The best time to invest was 20 or 30 years ago. The next best time is *now*—the decision to invest is a no-brainer. All of history shows that investing is the way to win. So be a winner.

## SMART WOMAN STRATEGIES

A smart woman understands what constitutes an investment:

- ♀ She would spread her risk by investing in different assets—by diversifying.
- ♀ She would start to learn more about the different kinds of investment.
- ♀ She would invest through funds until she felt confident to invest directly.
- ♀ Generally, she would leave her investments alone, knowing it costs her every time she buys and sells.

# PART V

# YOUR INVESTMENT TEAM

# 22
# PUTTING YOUR TEAM TOGETHER

You may be in charge of your financial future, but you don't have to do it all on your own. No matter how organised you are or how well-disciplined you become, you will need expert help from time to time. It is important to surround yourself with a team of professionals who will assist you to make good decisions and provide good advice.

We all need some help and advice from time to time, but when you're dealing with your finances, talk to the professionals. No matter how hard you work at learning what you need to know, you will never be as informed or up to date as you need to be.

Your team needs to include one or more of the following:

*lawyer;*
*accountant;*
*real estate agent;*
*sharebroker;*
*tax specialist;*
*insurance broker;*
*investment adviser;*
*trust lawyer.*

The level of professional help you need depends on your circumstances and what you are planning to do: the bigger your goals and the more complicated your affairs, the more advice you will need. If your affairs are fairly straightforward—for example, if you have a mortgage and earn some dividends—a general accountant will be able to help you file your tax return and minimise your tax liabilities. However, if you have several rental properties, own your own business or have become involved in trading shares, you will need an accountant with a degree of specialisation. Other people who have invested in the same things as you should be able to recommend someone experienced and appropriate and it is usually easy to find a property investment association or share investment group to join.

Remember that your adviser is working for you and you are paying for their service. If you are not satisfied, get a new one. Your financial self-sufficiency and security are far too important to be stymied by an inadequate or incompetent adviser. As always, winners work with winners: ask the people whose achievements you respect for recommendations. Typically, once you find one good professional, they will be able to recommend others who can be of use to you—they too like to work with other good people. Ideally, you want to end up surrounded by a team of well-informed advisers who are all willing to work together to secure the best outcomes for you.

*Kerry runs a thriving delicatessen business specialising in local produce. She has several specialist advisers that she uses frequently. She has them all working well together to ensure that her business stays successful and that her personal finances continue in line with her plan. She makes sure they meet each other and talk regularly about her affairs.*

Kerry's team of advisers

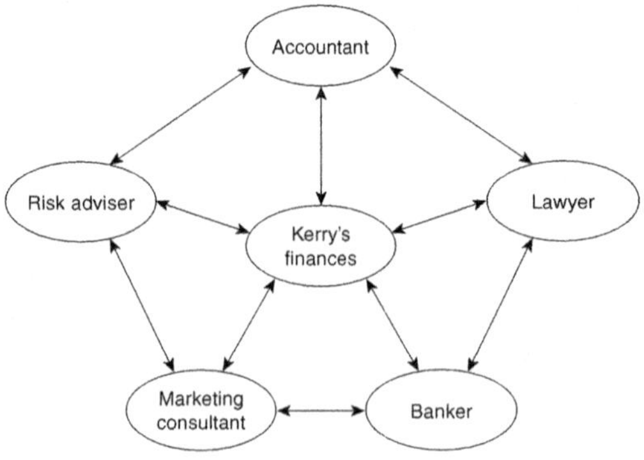

You need to look closely at which area you need the most help with. At any given time, it is probably easy to identify which area is holding you back. What is the one financial thing which, if dealt with, could transform your position? Different women will need different help at different times. One may need specialist help with the creation or management of a trust. Another may need help to clarify what it is that she is trying to achieve, to set goals and plans and to achieve these plans. If you are getting involved in property investment, you will want to focus on finding a good real estate agent, building a relationship with a trusted valuer, finding a reputable tax accountant and dealing with an effective mortgage broker.

If you own a business you also need specialist advisers. You might need a general business coach. Depending on what's important to the success of your business you may need some specialist consultants. You will need to perform superbly at whatever the most important aspect of the business is. If you are in retail, for example, your purchasing or your merchandising might be critical to your success. In another business, the most important function might be your marketing or your distribution. Whatever your business needs to excel at will determine what kind of specialist you need to find.

It can be expensive to hire good advisers. However, it will cost you even more if you receive poor advice or no advice at all. As with most things, you get what you pay for. You can make sure you get value for money by choosing your adviser with care. You will also need to brief them well so that you do not waste time (and your money). Make sure all of the information you need is available and brief them on your overall plans and objectives. Introduce them to other advisers in your team so that there is no double up.

> You can delegate authority to professionals to do certain things for you, but you cannot, and must not, delegate your responsibility for your finances and your future.

It is very hard for you to outperform the team—in other words, your success is unlikely to be greater than the team's performance. If you are serious, you will get a good team together and then take care to keep them working for you. And make them operate as a team. You can't go to sleep on the job and just assume that your accountant, financial planner and sharebroker will now take care of everything. It's your money and your life, so don't abdicate your role. Make sure you are at the centre of your team of professionals.

Never under-estimate the value of your network. The people you know and the people that they in turn know can make a huge difference to your success. All smart business people know this—that's why they spend so much energy catching up with and developing their networks. The web of people you know who will support you, teach you and advise you is invaluable. Some of this you clearly have to pay for, but you'll find you get lots more as well.

## CHOOSING PROFESSIONALS

Asking for recommendations from people you know and trust is the best way to find a good professional. There are two main rules to remember:

- ♀ *Good professionals do what's right for you—not what's right for them*. Even though your advisers are in business and have to earn a living, it is you—the client—who should come first. Sometimes that will mean telling you they can't help, sending your business away or advising you to do nothing (and therefore pay them little or nothing).
- ♀ *Good professionals advise you rather than sell to you*. One of the problems for many professionals (especially in the finance field) is that they only get paid if you buy, sell or change something, as they are paid for transactions or on commission. So it takes a very professional sharebroker to tell you to wait for a month or two.

> A key issue is to inquire how the professional is rewarded. Ask them whether they are paid by fee or commission. If by commission, it's in their interests to sell you something or they don't get paid. If by fee, it will cost you no matter what you decide to do, but the adviser has no reason to steer you in the direction of anything that is not right for you. And there is no conflict of interest. There is really no right answer, but it is better for you to know where you stand from the start.

You need to understand how the system works and take care both to choose well and to manage your team well. No one is perfect, and your advisers may make mistakes from time to time; it is therefore up to you to stay focused on managing your professionals.

How do you find your team? You could start by using the obvious criteria of qualifications and experience. But, as with finding all of the other professionals in your life, word of mouth is usually the best method. Ask around. Inquire about satisfaction and levels of service. Good people will lead you to other good people. Other questions that you should ask include:

*What are your qualifications?*
*What professional associations do you belong to?*
*Does your association have a code of professional conduct?*
*How do you get paid?*
*Are you affiliated with any other institution? Are you independent?*
*What research and support do you have access to?*
*What sort of services do you provide?*
*How do you work with clients?*
*How are complaints dealt with?*

Ultimately, you will have to trust your judgement, as any half-reasonable professional should pass the above tests. That's why recommendations are so useful. But you have to be comfortable with the person and find them easy to ask questions of and confide in. You are expecting to have a long-term relationship with each of your advisers, so choose with care.

## SMART WOMAN STRATEGIES

A smart woman would assemble the best possible team of advisers:

- ♀ She would decide what type of specialist help she needs to help her achieve financial independence.
- ♀ She would find some people who fit these roles by asking for recommendations.
- ♀ She would interview professionals to ensure she could work effectively with them and they could form a team.
- ♀ She would find out how they get paid.
- ♀ She would then get them to work as her 'dream team' to ensure she achieves her plans.
- ♀ She would manage them well—after all, it's her money and financial future at stake!

# PART VI

# MONEY AND RELATIONSHIPS

# 23
# MONEY AND RELATIONSHIPS

Money problems can kill a lot of relationships. It is up to you not to let it kill yours. Relationships can also 'kill' a woman's money—so make sure that doesn't happen either!

Money is a very powerful factor in relationships. It determines the lifestyle you have as a couple, where you live and often what you do and whom you associate with. Money can be a source of strife and disagreement between couples—counsellors and surveys report that couples fight about money more than anything else.

Whether or not they're aware of it, women share full responsibility for the results of any joint financial decisions their partner makes. A woman in a relationship will be jointly liable for any debts that are incurred, for example.

Relationships can, of course, be extremely good for your finances and your net worth. Two can live more cheaply, for a start. It is much easier to buy a home and work to accumulate net worth if there are two of you working. Two people who share a dream about their lives together have a huge amount of energy and commitment to making that dream come true. They support each other—and their love for each other keeps them on track with the plan. In addition, you have the knowledge and skill of the other person to draw on—you don't have to do it all alone.

It is not a good idea—for either your relationship or your financial position—to only discuss money (acrimoniously) when the bank statement arrives, the credit card bill comes or you find the ATM is no longer giving out money. Loving each other is not enough when it comes to managing money. And poor money management can mean the end of love sooner rather than later. It isn't going to work any better just because you don't talk about it. In fact, not discussing it, not having a shared plan and not working together to use each other's skills is usually just a recipe for being poor.

The problem with couples is that there are two of you. Whether you are in an established relationship or contemplating a life with someone else, it is worth spending some time thinking about your differing approaches to money.

All relationships include differences—they can be very appealing, exasperating or downright infuriating. But when it comes to money, they can be very serious indeed.

I rarely find that individuals in a relationship have a similar approach to money. Usually spenders are attached to savers, considered folk have found someone impulsive attractive, well-informed individuals have a partner who knows zilch about finance, and those who know where every penny goes are married to someone who has no idea. Risk-takers and daredevils often love someone who is risk averse, those who are well-grounded in today's realities are attracted to someone whose eye is on the distant future and the laid back move in with the obsessives!

How does your (prospective) partner see money? You have already spent some time considering your money habits and the influence your background and upbringing have had on your approach. But your partner's past matters too. He or she may have grown up in a very different sort of family with a very different approach. Your partner's parents may have discussed money openly, or even fought often and bitterly over money. All of this history is already in your relationship. It pays to understand what money baggage your partner is carrying. In very practical ways, these attitudes will influence each of your views about whose role it is to deal with money, how comfortable you each feel about debt, what your attitude to saving and investing is, and how you handle money on a daily basis.

Women often find out the hard way that there is a big gulf of understanding between them and their partner over money. This is often hidden in the early stages of relationships. At the beginning, every difference is a delight rather than a problem.

Young people in particular can be oblivious to huge differences between them—often neither of them has much and the only thing they have to focus on is getting through each day as it comes. But, as earnings increase and other responsibilities like mortgages and children arrive, the gulf can loom large and come as a big surprise.

There is less excuse for those of us who form relationships at a later age. Some women will have several live-in relationships over a lifetime. But money is still a taboo subject for many. We are still inclined to view discussion of money as highly unromantic and even a little grubby. We also fear being seen as too eager to assess a potential partner's financial situation. Again, all too often the difficulty is dealt with by silence.

It is important to look closely at your partner's money attitudes and habits around money. Ask your partner about some of his or her experiences around money in childhood and adolescence. Do the money habits test together—it will be fun to compare results.

You do not need to be the same in your approach to money, and it doesn't particularly matter if you are quite opposite. What *does* matter is that you each understand where the other is coming from and that there is some commitment to a shared approach to money within the relationship.

## SMART WOMAN STRATEGIES

A smart woman would give some serious thought to her partner's money personality:

- ♀ She would ask about her partner's circumstances when he or she was a child. Was the family well-off or poor? Was money an issue?
- ♀ She would find out what her partner remembers about how money was dealt with in his or her family. Who played what role? Were there fights about money?
- ♀ She would observe how her partner approaches money as an adult.

- ♀ She would listen to her partner's views about money.
- ♀ She would complete the money habits test with her partner and compare results.

# 24
# HONEY, LET'S TALK ABOUT OUR MONEY

Married or not, in an established relationship or just thinking about one, you should have some strategies for getting your partner to talk about money and your finances. Many women tend to avoid this—we are often afraid of conflict. If we don't talk about it there won't be a fight. Correct. But when the fight does come, we could end up broke.

Many couples deal with this difficult subject by ignoring it—not dealing with it at all. This is not only unhealthy for the relationship, but it can lead to devastating results in terms of your financial position.

One of the most important things I do in my work is to get a couple to talk about their finances and how they deal with them—this can often be the first real discussion about money that they have had in 20 years (other than arguments about it). But you cannot ignore your finances just because it is difficult to deal with them within your relationship. The results of the choices you are making together—or separately—will eventually impact on you both whether you are still together or not.

At some level, we commit to our partners 'for richer or poorer', as the saying goes. But believe me, richer is much better! The price for not tackling the money issue with your partner may be very high—even bankruptcy.

No partners who run a business together would think it was OK to never talk about the business. Yet that's what your personal finances are—the money 'business' of your shared life. It's even harder when neither of you has had good role models when growing up—if you have never seen two responsible adults plan their finances and deal well with each other about money, then it can be hard to know where to start. Even worse, some of your own experiences growing up or in earlier relationships may have been less than pleasant, so you may feel very reluctant to step into the ring.

I can only encourage you to break this very destructive cycle. Do it for yourself. Do it for the relationship. Do it for your children (for their futures as well as by being a good role model). You probably have a lot of living left to do, so determine that it's going to be a good life and that you are going to ensure that it is financially secure.

Talking about your family finances with your partner is a way of loving and caring for each other. You will know each other well enough to have some good ideas about how to open up the conversation without presenting an argument or seeming to criticise or complain. Men (especially older ones) are often very sensitive to any implied criticism that they don't 'provide' well enough, as many were brought up to shoulder that responsibility alone for the family. Younger men and women tend to expect a partner to carry the financial load more equally.

It can be easier to begin very positively and to talk about dreams and goals for the future. When you are able to say, 'What you want is very important to me . . .' you are off to a very good start. I am, of course, assuming that you have a good relationship. If not, then perhaps sorting out your financial future together is not your first priority.

If you both want many of the same things in your life, you can move to planning your money in line with those goals. If you want very different things, then you have more talking to do and more negotiation about what each of you gets to do from your individual list. Clearly, the earlier in your relationship these discussions take place the better.

The next step is to begin to operate like a team. Blame has no place in this process—it's about where you go from here rather than what sins have been committed in the past. Apologies for past transgressions are always a good idea—but apologies work best when you make them first before expecting them from others.

If you can agree that you have shared dreams and goals for the future and that each of you should be able to get some of what you want, then you have a good basis to begin planning how to make this happen no matter what has gone wrong in the past.

The other things that are worth talking about are your individual and joint skills. Couples tend to have different experiences, preferences and skills. If you use these well, you'll be in a much better position than either of you alone. A good place to start is to acknowledge what you know the other person is good at. These are strengths that could be used to plan and progress your financial position. People feel much more positive if they feel competent. Within the partnership, you are likely to have a wide range of skills and abilities to address your finances. As much as possible, try to enlist the strengths and competencies of the other person. I usually find that each person in a couple will do the hard work for the other even when they would be reluctant to do it alone. Such is the power of love.

Here are some questions that may help in structuring and guiding your discussion. It's a good idea for each of you to take turns answering the questions. Make sure you listen to the other person with respect and without interrupting—otherwise the conversation is sure to be over quickly!

*What do you dream of in our life together?*
*How do you want us to live in the future?*
*What plans do you have for children and family?*
*How long do you plan to work?*
*What would make you happy in retirement?*
*Where will we live when we are retired?*
*What will we do when we are older?*
*How much income do you want in retirement?*
*How do you feel about how we deal with money?*
*How satisfied are you with our current income?*
*How much do we owe?*
*How do you feel about our current level of debt?*
*How do you feel about how we spend our money?*
*What do you think we should spend less on?*
*What do you think we should spend more on?*
*What do you think our combined net worth is?*

*How do you feel about our rate of progress?*
*How satisfied are you with what we save?*
*Have we enough to cover emergencies?*
*How do you feel about our investment progress?*
*How do you feel about your prospects at work?*
*How do you feel about my prospects at work?*
*Are you satisfied with what we are doing to earn more income?*
*What do you really want that we can't afford?*
*How do you feel about managing money?*
*What aspects of our finances are you comfortable with managing?*
*What things to do with money do you feel good at?*
*What aspects of money management do you think I am good at?*
*How well do you think we share our family finance management?*

## SMART WOMAN STRATEGIES

A smart woman would initiate conversations about money:

- ♀ She would ask about her partner's dreams and goals for the future.
- ♀ She would share some of her own dreams and goals.
- ♀ She would use the above questions to open up the discussions on money in her partnership.

# 25
# AVOIDING STDs—SEXUALLY TRANSMITTED DISASTERS

There are many positive aspects to relationships, such as shared love and mutual support. However, just as you are affected positively by all of the good things your partner may do, you are also affected negatively by any mistakes or poor decisions that he or she may make. Some of these could have a disastrous effect on your finances.

Some of the things you need to be aware of and protect yourself against include:

- ♀ *Debts*. As a couple, your debts are shared just like your assets. You are likely to be aware of joint commitments like the mortgage on your home, but might be unaware of gambling debts or the fact that your partner has borrowed against your home to fund a (failing) business. You can't insure against this kind of behaviour, but you do need to stay awake. Your home loan should be joint and it should require both of your signatures to change. The same goes for any of your other investments and assets.
- ♀ *Poor ownership structures*. I quite often come across couples who own all of their assets in their own names. This is not a problem if all you're talking about is a home and a car. But if it includes rental properties, a business, and so on, you run the risk of a disaster in one area (a failing business, a sudden drop in the property market, loss of employment) affecting all of your assets. This will happen because your creditors (to whom you or the business owe money) can go after each and every asset you own until they get all of

their money. This could extend to the family home and personal possessions, and ultimately take you to bankruptcy. Take care to separate high-risk activities like businesses or property development from the rest of your assets.

- *Guarantees*. You may be asked by the bank to give personal guarantees for a loan. Banks don't usually release these guarantees easily. You may unwittingly sign away all of your hard-won security. Believe it or not, it is not that hard to make lots of money. Many couples have done this through a family-owned business. But the attrition rate is high—and many couples lose everything. It can be very tempting to use the family home to raise money for a business or other investment. Know your bottom line—you may need to keep some things sacred, such as the family home. It may be better to keep some assets in your own name and far removed from any risky ventures your partner may be engaged in—and small businesses *are* risky. Family trusts can also provide protection for family assets to separate them from other ventures.
- *Having no income*. It is unlikely that a single woman will have no income unless she is temporarily unemployed, caring for small children or on a sickness benefit for a time. However, women in relationships all too often have no income for many years. This is usually by choice, as their partner's income may be sufficient for both of them or they are absent from the workforce for years to bring up small children. If anything happened to their relationship, or even if their partner were killed, they may be left with no income in such circumstances—and might find it very hard to reestablish a reasonable income. Guard against such a disaster through insurance for death or disability. If you choose not to work, it is also worth trying to ensure that your skill set does not become obsolete.
- *Separation and divorce*. While this is always a difficult time, it does not have to be a financial disaster. The law requires that assets are split reasonably evenly. However,

you do need to be aware that many people tuck money and assets away in advance of leaving a relationship. So I'll say it again: you need to take an active role in the management of the family finances and you need to know what is where and what is happening to your money at all times. It can be incredibly difficult to uncover these sorts of activities after the event and may be so expensive that you cannot afford to pursue the matter. Beware of joint bank accounts that hold a lot of cash—it is not uncommon for one partner to empty such an account before they leave.

If you come into the relationship with many more assets than your partner, you need to be aware of how the law will regard this property if your relationship fails. You may want to consider protecting those assets through a property agreement or a trust.

Separation occurs for all kinds of reasons other than money. However, once a couple separates, the battles over money intensify. This is not a good time to find out that you have been living in cloud cuckoo land where your finances are concerned. Even a partner who has been very easy to deal with until now, and who has behaved very responsibly with money up to this point, can become very antagonistic. It is not a good time for you to have to learn the basics—and you may need some very expensive help to dig yourself out of a position that you need never have been in.

Over the years, I've found that men are often better prepared for these disasters, especially men whose partners have allowed them to control the family finances. Not only do they know where the money is, they may be the one who has the relationships with the accountant, lawyer, trustees and everyone else who matters to your finances. From a woman's point of view this is not a smart arrangement. You owe it to yourself to be aware of any and all aspects of your finances, joint as well as personal. That's the best time to think about future problems and take the right steps to offset the risks to your future financial self-sufficiency.

## SMART WOMAN STRATEGIES

A smart woman would ensure she understands how money works in her relationship:

- ♀ She would make sure she was fully informed about family finances.
- ♀ She would not turn over the responsibility for joint money to anyone else.
- ♀ She would ensure that her signature is required for any change to loans, etc.
- ♀ She would avoid signing any guarantees.
- ♀ She would ensure she understands any documents she signs.

# 26
# GETTING YOUR FINANCES SORTED—TOGETHER

You may have done quite a bit of this already for yourself—either because you have been single or because you alone took the initiative within your relationship. However, sorting your joint finances is a little more complicated.

As you begin to work together on your joint finances, there are five principles you will find useful.

1. *Focus on the positive aspects of your money*. It's all too easy for everything about money and finance to seem like a chore and to be negative. Instead, it's better to focus on what better teamwork and money management can do for each partner and for the family as a whole. After all, this is not about money: it's about what you can be, do and have together as a family and separately as individuals. Money is just a means to an end. Nearly everyone is interested enough in something or has some dreams they want to fulfil. The trick with this is to show the other, perhaps reluctant, person how they can get some of what they want in life by giving their finances some attention. This might be a holiday, a lower workload, a home or the opportunity to explore an education or a particular area of interest. You will know the person well and should use that insight to help your partner focus on how life could change for the better with some adjustments to the way you approach your finances.
2. *It takes two to get the family finances straight*. A woman needs to take care of her own financial position irrespective of her partner, but if she is in a relationship, then it is in the whole

family's interests that both adults are working together to ensure the best outcomes for everyone. It's best to start saying 'we' instead of 'you' or 'I'.

3 *Set some ground rules for how you go about tackling your finances.* The most important one is to agree that you will not 'blame' each other for whatever has happened to date. People who feel attacked will simply defend or counter-attack, which won't help you get anywhere with your finances.
4 *Stick to the facts.* Both parties should try to be as unemotional as they can—even if the emerging picture is pretty horrible. Again, you have to keep your eye on the bigger picture—presumably you want to get an improvement in the money situation and you also want to remain in the partnership.
5 *'Get real' about the way things are.* In other words, you need to be as honest about your financial situation as possible. Get everything out of the closet and onto the table. It is in everyone's interest that you know exactly where you are starting from—it's very disheartening if, over the coming months, more bad stories keep popping up.

This is the time to do a net worth statement for the family. The net worth statement will show you what the family's financial position is at the moment. It will show you what you own together and also reveal the debts you have together. Women are often unaware that they have joint responsibility for family debt—even if they did not take out the loan.

You will also want to do an income statement so that you are both very clear about how much money is coming into the family each year.

Couples tend to find it very useful to both track expenditure over a few weeks or months using a notebook to record every spend. When I sit down with couples at the end of a week or month to analyse their notebooks, they are usually astonished to see where their money goes. Expenditure is often an area of great conflict—you may have differing priorities for consumption, differing interests, differing expectations. But sharing these expenditure habits (and they may have been well hidden until now) is a very necessary step—if you don't know what is happening to the family money at the moment, it is impossible to plan for changes to get a better outcome. Individuals are usually surprised to see their own spending patterns—and they are often amazed (and angered) at their partner's. But if you are going to operate as a partnership, you will need to work together on this—and sensitively.

When you have done all this work together, you will be in a good position to plan for change. You may need some support with this, but basically you'll need to agree on some guiding principles for family money, such as:

*We'll save X per cent of our income.*
*We'll live on $X per week.*
*We'll only borrow for certain things—like a mortgage.*
*We'll pay bills on or before the due date, including everything on the credit card.*
*We'll use all our savings initially to clear our debts and then we'll look at other investments.*

## SMART WOMAN STRATEGIES

A smart woman would work closely with her partner to plan the family finances for the future:

- ♀ She would gather up the information and documents she needs, including a recent bank statement, credit card bills, etc.
- ♀ She would agree on some rules—like sticking to the facts and not criticising each other for what has happened until now. This is about the future, not the past.
- ♀ She would take time to talk about what she and her partner want and what they want together, then begin the process of allocating money to these dreams and goals.

# 27 MAKING MONEY WORK FOR BOTH OF YOU

It is very important that both you and your partner are equally involved in planning and managing your finances. You cannot afford to take the risk of leaving your finances to the management of another person, no matter how trusted or beloved. No law forces him to do a competent job on the family money or to take financial responsibility for you for the rest of your life. You are deemed to be a fully knowledgeable and responsible adult where your family finances are concerned and you can't delegate away this responsibility. And you'd be crazy to. So don't end up taking responsibility for the household accounts while your partner takes responsibility for saving and investment. If you wouldn't let someone run your life, why would you let them run your finances? Couples who have been together for a long time or who have been very busy bringing up a family often cope by separating their roles and making one partner responsible for the family finances. But this means the other partner loses control of their financial well-being. It's your life, and you can organise it any way you like but I wouldn't give anyone else control of my financial well-being. If you mess it up, through neglect or otherwise, no one is coming to the rescue.

There are several other financial aspects to consider, particularly if you are in a new relationship, second marriage or blended family. Many people enter new relationships with very different levels of wealth. This is far less likely in first relationships, as most of us have little or nothing to our name in the early years. However, by the time people are in their thirties or forties they may have considerable assets or debts (or both).

If you are entering a new relationship, you will need to

consider this. Given the way that the law generally works, the new partner may have a claim on your property if the relationship survives for three years or longer. You might, for example, own your own house. You worked very hard as a single woman to pay off the mortgage and are proud of your achievement. Or it might have been purchased from your share of your divorce settlement. Your new partner moves in with you and you live together for four years. You separate after a monumental row. He files a claim for some of the value of your house—and he's entitled to.

There are various ways to address issues such as this. One is a pre-nuptial agreement if you are to be married. Or you can draw up a property-sharing agreement. You agree what each is bringing into the relationship and who gets what if the relationship ends. However, many people feel very uncomfortable with the idea of pre-nuptial or property-sharing agreements—they can seem most unromantic, even downright distrustful of your intended.

Yet another way to protect your assets is to take care not to allow them to become relationship property by not using them within the relationship. While this is clearly impossible with a family home, it would be relatively easy with a rental property or a parcel of shares—you would keep such an asset separate, account for it separately and not use the rental income or dividends as family money. A family trust may be useful.

The detail of these arrangements is well beyond the scope of this book. However, the point is that you do need to consider these issues if you are entering a new relationship and if you have significant assets. I have come across several women who have had their assets reduced by a series of relationships—they may have come out of their first marriage with a reasonable settlement which they worked hard to build into a secure position. Then a new relationship foundered and their assets were halved again. It is clearly possible for this to happen several times to the unwary.

You will also need to take care that joint assets are titled properly in your new relationship. If you move into his house and start to contribute to mortgage payments, you need to be careful that the house is not still in your partner's ex-wife's name. I recently worked with a woman who saw her partner's ex-wife entitled to most of his estate following his death, as much of the necessary paperwork was never amended. Women often assume that, because this is not fair, it can't happen—but you are deemed a responsible adult in law and it is up to you to see that wills, trusts, insurances, and so on detail the right people as beneficiaries or owners. You also need to keep very good records.

This is one area where professional advice is essential. In the case of new relationships when there are considerable assets involved, it is advisable for each of you to have separate legal advice. You should also consider maintaining separate lawyers—if things get difficult in the future, it is unhelpful for you to have to find a new lawyer if your family lawyer acts for your partner.

You should complete all the necessary documents together and make sure that they say what you want them to say. And never sign anything you do not understand. Any lawyer or accountant worth their fee should be able to provide a plain English version of your documents. Remember, it's your life and your future financial position that's at stake.

## SMART WOMAN STRATEGIES

A smart woman would consider the financial implications of a new relationship:

- ♀ If there was a big difference between her net worth and that of her new partner, she would find out how to protect her finances against a future breakdown in the relationship.
- ♀ She would check that all of the legal documents affecting her say what they need to say and specify the right people as beneficiaries and owners—including wills, trusts, insurances and bank accounts.

# 28
# MINE, YOURS AND OURS

Couples whose relationship was formed when they were relatively young or couples who have been together for a long time usually have all of their finances merged—out of habit as much as anything else.

However, it is not unusual for couples in a new relationship to have big differences in their net worth, incomes or both. In addition, one or both partners may have children from a previous relationship. This can provide a quite difficult set of financial circumstances. When one partner has had a difficult separation or divorce, or feels very poorly treated in a financial sense by their former spouse, they may be very wary of how finances are handled in the new relationship. In addition, there may be issues over children. What are the responsibilities of a new partner to the children of the other? Both may have children, but quite different patterns may have been set about schooling, pocket money, treats, etc. And there will still be all of the necessary connections with ex-partners about contributions to and maintenance for children. It can be a minefield.

You need to think about how you will deal with this fairly. Who should pay for what? What expenses are legitimate 'we' expenses? One solution is to have three pools of money in the family—'our' money, 'your' money and 'my' money. This may seem unromantic, but it is a very practical solution and provides a way for each partner to maintain some independence and avoid fights over what constitutes legitimate expenses. At the very least, it smoothes the path during a 'shakedown' period in the new family. We are all grappling with the changes these new models of 'family' are bringing—and, of course, we are struggling with how to organise our lives and our finances to fit. The old ways don't seem to provide much help.

You can do a plan or budget for 'our' money as you normally would. Decide what living expenses are covered from this pool, agreeing on limits for each category. You will also need to agree on how much each of you contributes to this—one of you may have far higher income or may 'own' several of the children. Again, there's no right formula for doing this—it is each couple's decision. But it is better to make these decisions than to constantly bicker over who spent what and who had to pay for it.

Some couples award each partner an 'allowance' which can be spent at their discretion—on outings, presents, hobbies, and so on. Others may simply decide that what is not pooled as joint money is the individual's to retain and spend or invest as desired.

Strategies such as these can be useful ways of getting around an individual's natural desire to maintain some independence, especially if they have been used to living alone for some time.

While you might choose to make separate investments, there is clearly a case for joint savings and investments as well—after all, if you are expecting to be together in the future you will want to make provision for the future financial position of your family unit.

It is also a good idea to set aside an emergency fund for the family—as a rule of thumb, you will need at least three months' worth of expenses at hand to cover illness, accidents or loss of employment.

It is relatively easy for a couple to run a joint bank account as well as individual accounts, and for each partner to make automatic payments to this on an agreed basis.

## SMART WOMAN STRATEGIES

A smart woman would consider how to handle money within the new relationship:

- ♀ She would agree with her partner about what each should contribute to the family pool.

- ♀ She would also agree on a budget for saving and investing, spending, and so on.
- ♀ Finally, she and her partner would agree on personal spending.

# 29
# HANDLING AN INHERITANCE

It has often been said that there are only three legitimate ways of creating wealth:

- earning it;
- marrying it; and
- inheriting it.

It may sound like a dream come true to find that you have been left money by someone else, but inheritances can be very problematic for women.

Receiving an inheritance is much more common than you might at first think. Women are often younger than their male partners and so often outlive them. There are many 'wealthy widows', and many of them are relatively young.

In addition, the baby boomer generation is in the process of inheriting from the World War II and Depression generation. Parents, aunties, uncles and godparents are passing on and leaving their money to us. That generation was frugal and believed in the creation of wealth for future generations. As a result, many of these legacies are large. The recent surge in property values worldwide has meant that even inheriting a modest property hitherto considered to be of little value may represent a significant inheritance. Internationally, we are witnessing the largest transfer of wealth that the world has ever seen.

When a woman receives a legacy she faces several emotional issues:

- ♀ It may be the first 'serious' lump of money that she has ever had, which can be quite a shock.
- ♀ Even a modest inheritance can change the life of the inheritor. Any big change in your life, even a good one, nearly always brings emotional disruption as well.
- ♀ She may feel very guilty about having inherited wealth—she may feel she did nothing to earn it or to create it through her own efforts.
- ♀ Someone is dead—perhaps it was someone she cared about a great deal. In any case, she may feel very bad about benefiting from someone else's death even if that is what the person wanted.
- ♀ There is nothing like an inheritance to bring out bad behaviour in various friends and family members. Many will be resentful of her changed circumstances and envious of her good fortune. It is not unusual for family members to be very angry about the will of the deceased. This can often dredge up old grievances and reignite family feuds.
- ♀ Inheritances bring us close to the subject of death. A legacy can often mean we are now in the front line and can't pretend we are children who will live forever any more. When this is added to grief for a loved one, it can be very unsettling.

Any woman receiving an inheritance needs to seek out good advice and decide what to do with it. There is often pressure to rush off, make decisions and change everything all at once. But this is actually a time to do nothing for a while. There may be people—some well-meaning and others not—who are urging you to sell, invest or spend. There is rarely any need for urgent action and you should take plenty of time to consider your options and the changes to your life that this money may bring. Don't rush. Give it six to twelve months. Promise yourself that you won't make any decisions until you feel you're ready and have taken plenty of time.

It's also important to take time to grieve. If you were close to the person who has willed you an inheritance, you may be greatly affected by their death. The grieving process is neither well-understood nor accorded much time in our society. But we do know it takes time. You should not be making major decisions that involve life changes or great amounts of money when you are still in an emotional state.

It's important to get good advice. You will probably need help from a lawyer, an accountant, a financial planner and perhaps a risk adviser. You may already have a good working relationship with one of these who could act on your behalf in pulling a 'network' of advisers together. Or you may be meeting these advisers for the first time. It is important that you take your time, find someone you are comfortable with and make no decisions until you are sure you understand everything. There are no prizes for speed here.

No one may know about your inheritance—and you are not obliged to tell anyone. Women often create a great deal of unnecessary trouble for themselves and expose themselves to lots of unsolicited advice by telling people far and wide about their inheritance. Just as with a Lotto win—or a bad debt—this is your business and you may prefer to be silent on the subject.

Women have a frightening tendency to give away the money they inherit—even if they are in dire need of it. Women I see often feel 'guilty' at their good fortune and feel that they should rescue (or compensate) others. You are especially vulnerable in the early days, particularly if you are awash with grief as well. If, on reflection and after considerable time, you wish to make gifts to others, then that is your right and choice. However, it is important that you do not feel pressured into it in the heat of the moment.

Above all, explore your options. Even a relatively modest investment can make a great difference if it is well invested. You could choose to repay debt, buy a home, get an education, change career path or ensure retirement security. But unless the inheritance is very large, you probably can't do all of these so choices have to be made. If you have never spent much time considering what you really value in life, then you will need to do some careful thinking here.

Receiving an inheritance is good fortune even though you may have mixed feelings. However, it can pose many issues and choices for the inheritor. It is often an unexpected event and accompanied by a great deal of emotion—all difficult circumstances in which to make sound financial decisions.

Despite the grief that may be involved, inheriting as a widow is relatively straightforward from a financial viewpoint. Property you held jointly, such as your home, comes into your full ownership. You may also be the recipient of large amounts of insurance money or investments.

Women who are in a relationship will need to consider another dimension to inheritance. If you do not use the inheritance to buy a house or boat that you use within the family, the total inheritance remains yours and your partner has no claim on it if the relationship ends. You could also choose to invest your inheritance in several ways; as long as you do not use the proceeds (interest, rentals or dividends) as family money, your inheritance is safe against claims from your partner.

Some women reading this will be appalled—this sounds so calculating and mercenary. But not all relationships are well-established, and some that have been going for some time will be very rocky. Even the best relationship can founder.

*Helen is 25. She's a smart girl and is in her first job as a sales rep. Helen did a degree in marketing so she seems to have a good future, though at present nearly all of her savings are going to repay her student loan. As yet she has few assets. She lives in a cute rented cottage with Tim, her boyfriend of eighteen months. Tim is the same age. He has only just finished his studies as he spent a few years overseas. He has a good job in his sights.*

*Helen's dad has just died after a long illness. Her mother was killed years before in a car accident. As the only child, Helen has inherited $500,000 from her father's estate.*

*Her landlord wants to sell the cottage. Helen would love to own it. Tim wants her to buy it. What should she do?*

It's pointing out the obvious to say that Helen and Tim are very young and the relationship is of short duration. If Helen buys the house and they live in it together it will become relationship property. No doubt, Helen and Tim will work on the property together and spend money renovating it. If the relationship lasts for another eighteen months, Tim would have a claim on half the property if they were to split up. It can be hard to believe that someone you love and who loves you would do that—but if the relationship founders, love is unlikely to be the dominant emotion. And few people behave very well when there are hundreds of thousands of dollars at stake. Helen needs to be aware of this when she makes her decision. And she needs good professional advice.

## SMART WOMAN STRATEGIES

A smart woman would consider how to deal with her inheritance:

- She wouldn't rush. There is no hurry.
- She would decide whether she wanted to share the news or not.
- She would take time to grieve if the person was close to her.
- She would consider her dreams and goals for the rest of her life.
- She would seek out good advice.
- She wouldn't feel guilty—it's her money and it could be life-changing.
- She would consider whether or not to keep the inheritance separate within her relationship.

# 30 TRIPS AND TRAPS

As you go forward on your journey to having the life you want and ensuring that you have the money you'll need to fund it, there are a few things you need to watch out for.

Many wise women have found that it is very easy to sabotage themselves. I find that the same things come up again and again as derailers for women who are striving for self-sufficiency and financial independence.

It starts in our heads: no sooner have we resolved what we want and how we're going to make it happen than the inner voices of doubt begin. This is partly due to our early conditioning about money. When you begin to feel that the effort of financial self-sufficiency is all too much, remind yourself that it takes as least as much effort to be poor—and it's far less pleasant than independence. When you think that there's no point in wanting what you can't afford, ask yourself whether you want it enough to make it happen—and believe me, if the answer is 'yes', you can and will make it happen. Smart women have found that the biggest battle they have to fight for their happiness and their self-sufficiency is in their own heads.

There are some other traps on the way to independence:

♀ *The mortgage*. One very big trap is taking too long to pay off your mortgage. The reason I have singled this out is that the longer you take to pay it off, the more interest you will pay in total. This is such a big investment in your independence and self-sufficiency that it needs to be done well or it will undermine the other businesses of your life that you want to invest time, money and energy in. So pay it off as fast as possible. A relatively small increase in your monthly payment will mean that you pay the loan off faster and so save yourself a lot of money.

| Loan | Interest | Monthly payment | Years | Total paid |
|---|---|---|---|---|
| $250,000 | 7% | 1,938.25 | 20 | $465,179.36 |
| $250,000 | 7% | 1,766.95 | 25 | $530,084.40 |

In this example, the difference in the total interest paid is $64,905.04. This was achieved by paying $171.30 extra each month so that the loan was paid off in 20 years. You save a lot of money by paying off the loan as fast as you can, either by increasing your monthly payments or paying in lump sums you receive like bonuses, pay rises or inheritances.

One solution is to borrow less to begin with—in other words, settle for a home of lesser value. That way, you will be able to pay back the loan faster. Go back to your values—if the home is meeting the values you have around security, family and independence, then a $250,000 home may be just as good as a $500,000 one.

The interest rate that you pay also makes a very big difference. For example, a mortgage of $120,000 at 8 per cent over 25 years means you pay interest of $157,853, while a mortgage of $120,000 at 7.5 per cent over 25 years means you pay interest of $146,036.

While this is not the place to go into a detailed discussion on managing your mortgage, the amount of borrowing is usually so great that you really do need to give it some attention and manage it very well. The importance of almost every other money decision will pale by comparison.

♀ *Things with engines.* Motor vehicles are another trap—together with your home, you may find that they absorb all the cash you can possibly earn. Unless these are essential to meeting your dreams and the businesses of your life, watch your spending here. I am singling these out because they are expensive and can prevent you from allocating any of your resources to other life projects that are really important to you. A further trap with vehicles is that it can be very tempting to buy them with borrowed funds. This debt can be at a higher interest rate than your home loan. You can add the additional debt to your home loan; however, if you do, you need to be aware that, unless you increase your monthly repayments, the loan will take much longer (years more) to pay off and will cost you a great deal more in interest. Another $10,000 or $20,000 can seem insignificant on top of the amount you have already borrowed, but you need to keep in mind that it will cost you. Banks will lend you the money easily—that's their job! But that does not make it a good idea.

As shown in the graph below, if you borrow more on your home loan (for a car or maybe to redo the kitchen), you will either have to increase your monthly payments to pay the loan off in the same time period (25 years) or the loan will take a lot longer to repay and so cost you a considerable amount in extra interest over the additional years.

Home loan repayments if you borrow more

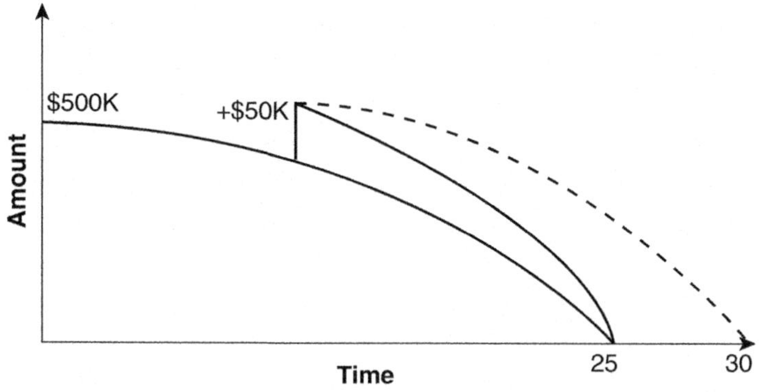


♀ *Holidays*. Travel is a very easy way to blow enormous amounts of money. Apart from travel costs and accommodation, we tend to have very loose controls on our spending when we tell ourselves we are on 'holiday'. So do your planning carefully here—you may want to prepare a specific budget for each one. Without ever leaving home, school holidays can fall into this category—many a smart woman has had her plans somewhat derailed by a houseful of teens over the holidays!

- ♀ *Credit cards*. How did we ever end up thinking that plastic was like free money? It's anything but free. You may buy things that are not in line with your plans or you may buy them before you can afford to pay for them. Interest rates on credit card debt are horrendous. If you know from experience that you are prone to splurges with the card, cut it up or leave it at home (for use in emergencies), or impose a cooling off period of 24 hours before you use it. It's so sad that a little piece of plastic can destroy the plans and lives of so many. Don't let it happen to you.

Each of us tends to have our own area of weakness when it comes to blowing the plan. What's yours? Eating out or grabbing takeaways is a real trap for working mums; clothes or shoes may be the single girl's trap; the mobile phone bill may be a monthly shock—and what about the groceries bought and dumped owing to poor meal planning? It's worth spending some time finding the one that's likely to derail you—you don't have to do everything perfectly, but it's worth picking off the big problems first.

A good friend, a coach or a mentor can be a great help to keep you on track with your plans and to help you avoid the trips and traps along the way.

## SMART WOMAN STRATEGIES

A smart woman would stay aware of the pitfalls for financial independence:

- ♀ If she decided to take on a mortgage, she would pay it off as quickly as possible.
- ♀ She would negotiate hard: every quarter of a per cent off her interest rate is worth a lot to her.
- ♀ Unless they were essential to her happiness, she would try not to have more house or motor vehicle than she needed—they'll just keep her poor.
- ♀ She would take great care with using her credit card.
- ♀ She would plan and budget well in advance for holidays.
- ♀ She would figure out what her weak spending spot was—and eliminate it.

# 31
# A LAST WORD TO SMART WOMEN

I could conclude by wishing you luck on the road to financial independence. But I don't think luck has anything to do with it.

Women become financially independent because they decide to. It's not necessarily an easy road to follow, but you can do it—and you will do it if you want to. You already have all of the intelligence and ability that you need. Reading this book must have convinced you that there is nothing especially complicated about finance. The only thing that's complicated is the jargon, and you'll soon be comfortable with that.

All the difficult stuff is about changing what's in your head and the effort of exchanging bad habits for good ones. But women take on huge challenges all the time—running households, bringing up children, re-entering the workforce, caring for ageing relatives, as well as earning a living. Learning a bit more about your money and how to manage it seems a minor challenge by comparison.

You should become financially free because it means you will have a much better life. The payoff is huge. And you are worth it.

## MORE GOOD BOOKS FROM ALLEN & UNWIN

Get Rich, Stay Rich . . . and Become Financially Free
Martin Hawes and Joan Baker

To be financially free is the ultimate goal—to be rich enough not to worry about money or work, and have little risk of losing your health.

A sensible investment strategy will help you achieve a comfortable lifestyle and a secure future, but it won't give you **financial freedom**.

So how do you become seriously wealthy? *Get Rich, Stay Rich* will help you develop the right attitude and skills to succeed in your quest for **financial freedom**. Start your journey to long-lasting wealth today!

Bestselling author and presenter MARTIN HAWES and business consultant JOAN BAKER provide individualised wealth coaching and seminars to help their clients become wealthy and free to pursue their dreams.

ISBN 1 74114 105 2

Printed in Dunstable, United Kingdom

91222213R00102